W9-CDO-281

DISCARD

THE PULLMAN
STRIKE
of 1894

THE PULLMAN
STRIKE
of 1894

Rosemary Laughlin

MORGAN
REYNOLDS
PUBLISHING
Greensboro, North Carolina

american workers

The Homestead Steel Strike of 1892

The Pullman Strike of 1894

The Ludlow Massacre of 1913-14

Mother Jones

THE PULLMAN STRIKE OF 1894

Library of Congress Cataloging-in-Publication Data

Laughlin, Rosemary.
    The Pullman strike of 1894 / Rosemary Laughlin.
    p. cm.
    Originally published: 2000 in the series Great events.
    Includes bibliographical references and index.
    ISBN-13: 978-1-931798-89-1 (library binding)
    ISBN-10: 1-931798-89-3 (library binding)
    1. Pullman Strike, 1894—Juvenile literature. 2. Strikes and
lockouts—Railroads—Juvenile literature. 3. Railroads—History—
Juvenile literature. 4. Labor movement—Illinois—Chicago—
Juvenile literature. [1. Pullman Strike, 1894. 2. Strikes and lock-
outs—Railroads. 3. Railroads—History. 4. Labor movement History.]
I. Title.
    HD5325.R121894 C5395 2006
    331.892'825230977311—dc22
                                            2005028637

Printed in the United States of America
First Edition

To Pat and Tony

CONTENTS

Chapter One
The Chicago Strike 11

Chapter Two
The Emergence of Unions 16

Chapter Three
A Company Town 26

Chapter Four
The Strike Spreads 39

Chapter Five
A Chain Reaction 64

Chapter Six
Debs Goes to Jail 80

Chapter Seven
The Commission's Report 95

Chapter Eight
Legacy 113

Timeline 124
Glossary 129
Sources 133
Bibliography 137
Web sites 140
Index 142

The Pullman Strike. (Courtesy of the Granger Collection.)

1.
The Chicago Strike

Worries and fears crackled like static electricity among the workers inside the Pullman Palace Car Company on the morning of May 11, 1894. Painters, seamstresses, car builders, steamfitters, electrical technicians, mechanics, wood trimmers, and assorted helpers all felt upset and anxious. They had reported to work but were unsure what would happen next. Rumors of a lockout circulated until, finally, union representatives told the workers to stop work, go outside, and vote on whether they wanted to strike. Like a giant wave, 3,000 workers laid down their tools and left the building. Three hundred remained inside, mostly clerks and foremen.

In a nearby meeting hall, the workers voted to strike. They did so because they felt there was no other way to convince George Pullman of their plight. For a year, their pay rates had steadily declined, and their work hours had been reduced, while the price of food and rent did not decrease. Their families were hungry and sick. They were simply not earning enough to live on.

Union rules required a vote of all members for a strike, which meant they would stop work—and receive no pay—until an agreement was made that would provide better working conditions upon their return.

Because of the hardship it created, a strike was a tactic of last resort. Before they voted to strike, workers had tried to discuss their concerns with Pullman. He told them business was bad and that he was keeping the factory open just to give them what work he could scrape up. But workers complained that Pullman officials, superintendents, and foremen had not seen their pay reduced. Stock dividends were still being paid to shareholders. When asked if he would allow a board of neutral judges to review the workers' complaints, Pullman refused.

On May 10, 1894, three of the employees who had brought the workers' concerns to Pullman were laid off. The rest feared that these three—there had been forty-six employee representatives in all—were being punished because of the requests they had made and for criticizing certain superintendents. They thought Pullman saw them as rebellious and threatening, and as the ringleaders of a strike movement. Later it would be clarified that the layoffs of these three were an unfor-

The Pullman Palace Car Company was headquartered twelve miles south of Chicago, a midwestern business hub. (Library of Congress)

tunate coincidence, but in the tension of the moment, the workers concluded they had been fired for speaking out.

The night of May 10, union representatives met to decide what to do. They were worried more workers might lose their jobs. This meeting lasted until five o'clock the next morning. The representatives agreed unity of action was essential and organized an election to vote about a possible strike.

The strikers then created a central committee that would meet daily in a public hall and act as a clearing-house for all problems. Food and medical services were already needed, and would now have to come from the charity of others. The response from church groups and sympathizers in Chicago was supportive and generous.

The committee's other major concern was violence. The strikers were committed to a peaceful solution and abhorred the possibility of vandalism or destruction at the Pullman plant by angry individuals or hoodlums from Chicago. Any violence would only hurt their cause by allowing Pullman to condemn the strikers for being an unruly mob. The committee organized three hundred strikers to set up twenty-four hour watches at various locations around the locked-up buildings.

This was the beginning of the Pullman Strike of 1894, also called the Chicago Strike. It lasted for two months

Until they were relieved by U.S. troops on July 6, 1894, a volunteer force of three hundred striking workers kept a twenty-four-hour watch on the Pullman plant to prevent violence or vandalism. Here they can be seen guarding the Arcade Building in Pullman, the equivalent of a modern-day mall. (Courtesy of the Chicago Public Library's Pullman Collection.)

and was full of unexpected and dramatic developments. Soon the direct effects of the strike would spread to twenty-seven states and territories. It was to become a landmark in the history of relations between workers and factory owners in the United States.

The Pullman Strike was a major battle between working people and corporation owners. President Grover Cleveland called it an "unusual and especially perplexing" affair, giving him the "most troublous and anxious" time during his administration. The strike proved that large numbers of sympathetic workers would actively support other workers who went out on strike. It also reflected the ongoing dispute between states' rights and federal powers, and defined new ways for state and federal governments to intervene in transportation and commerce.

How did this watershed disruption of the American economy come about? The best way to begin to understand the 1894 strike is to look at how the relationship between workers and management had developed in the decades after the Civil War.

2.
The Emergence of Unions

Before the Civil War, which lasted from 1861 to 1865, the standard working day in an American factory was at least ten hours for skilled workers and twelve to fourteen hours for unskilled laborers, including women and children. Few laws regulated workplace conditions, and dangerous, difficult jobs were common. After the Civil War, as American industry boomed, increasing numbers of workers were immigrants from overseas. They crowded into the slums of big cities like New York and Chicago, and their desperate need for work meant factory owners could pay them a pittance, knowing there were thousands more immigrants arriving every day.

As the workers became accustomed to life in America, learning the language and the customs, they also began

The influx of immigrants into American cities led to cramped, and often unsanitary, living conditions. (Library of Congress)

to band together in hopes of achieving better wages and working conditions. They realized the best, and perhaps the only, way to agitate successfully for better treatment from employers was to start unions. Unions are organized groups of workers that elect representatives to negotiate with management. During the first decades of structured labor in the United States, owners argued in court that unions were unconstitutional encroachments on their private property rights. But in 1842, in a case called Commonwealth v. Hunt, the Supreme Court ruled that labor unions were lawful organizations and that the strike was a legal weapon. By 1873, there were thirty national unions.

Early unions faced many challenges. They had few legal protections, which mean management could "bust" a union by punishing members until workers gave up in favor of keeping their jobs. Union representatives had to try to convince workers to accept their leadership and then convince management to negotiate. The only real leverage unions had was the threat of a walkout, or strike, and that could only succeed if management could be prevented from resuming business with temporary workers, often derisively called "scabs." When management wanted to bring in temporary workers, private guards, or even local or state troops, were often used to protect them. The threat of violence loomed over every conflict in the early years of American labor history.

The first major railroad strike began on the Baltimore & Ohio Railroad in 1877 after wages were repeatedly cut. The Baltimore & Ohio trains came to a halt, and angry mobs drove out the state troops that had been sent in to restore order. Sympathy strikes spread across the country, and soon the governors of Maryland, Illinois, Pennsylvania, and West Virginia asked for federal troops to help end the strike. It took two weeks to restore order and end the conflict.

Another strike, the so-called Haymarket Square riots of 1886, involved workers demanding an eight-hour work day at the McCormick reaper factory in Chicago. After three workers were killed by the police, anarchists and bystanders became involved. Their involvement resulted in a bomb and more deaths. This violence outraged the country.

In 1892, employees went on strike at the Carnegie

A barge burns on the Monongahela River during the Homestead riot near Pittsburgh, Pennsylvania, in 1892. (Courtesy of the Granger Collection.)

Steel Corporation in Homestead, Pennsylvania. Management planned to use the strike to break the union, hiring three hundred guards from the Pinkerton National Detective Agency to keep the workers out. When a gun battle began, the governor called out the militia. The result was a victory for Carnegie Steel. Only non-union men were hired to work at the mill after the Homestead Strike.

During these years of agitation, several leaders emerged in the union movement. Probably the most important was the cigar maker Samuel Gompers, who became president of his local union and then went on to found the American Federation of Labor (AFL) in 1881. Gompers avoided political entanglements, particularly with the increasingly popular socialist movement. Instead he stressed fundamental issues that were close to

Labor organizer Eugene V. Debs would play an essential role in the Pullman Strike. (Courtesy of the Granger Collection.)

the hearts of the AFL membership: higher wages, shorter hours, and more freedom to advance on the job.

Another influential man in labor unions would one day become the leader of America's socialist movement. Eugene Victor Debs was an idealist, a kind person, and an untiring worker for his beliefs. Though he was not a socialist at the time of the Pullman strike, he later became an unceasing advocate for that ideology.

Born in 1855 in Terre Haute, Indiana to French immigrant parents, Debs began working in railroad shops at the age of fifteen and later became a locomotive fireman. He joined the firemen's union, became a union officer, and was the editor of *Firemen's Magazine*. He was eventually elected city clerk in Terre Haute and became a member of the Indiana legislature.

Debs helped found the American Railway Union and was elected president on June 20, 1893. Its goal was to unite many different unions together to create one large union for all railroad workers. Unions were first formed to unite workers in a particular craft or skill. There were unions for locomotive engineers, firemen, brakemen, trainmen, baggage handlers, and others. The American Railway Union was an industrial union that accepted all kinds of workers from the least to the most skilled. This type of union is sometimes referred to as a vertical union.

One year after Debs became president, the American Railway Union had 150,000 members.

In April 1894, Debs and the American Railway Union gained national attention and recognition when James J. Hill of the Great Northern Railroad refused to increase the wages of his employees; at the time, they were the lowest paid on the transcontinental lines. The men of the Great Northern Railroad went on strike, and no trains moved on the Great Northern railroads except those carrying mail. (Because mail was a federal function, it was illegal for strikers to interfere with its delivery. Management often claimed that striking workers were disrupting the mail in their efforts to force federal intervention into a work stoppage.)

Debs, a powerful, persuasive speaker, addressed the strikers and urged discipline, cooperation, and nonviolence. His physical appearance—he was over six feet tall and clean shaven with strong features—enhanced his outgoing personality. His sincere speech was a success.

After Debs's speech, Hill agreed to a settlement arranged by the arbitration. The arbitrators—impartial judges brought in to settle a disagreement—agreed that wages should be increased, and they were—by a total of $146,000 a month. The strike was over in eighteen days. The union had won.

Debs was ecstatic over the agreement. To him this was proof that workers and managers could cooperate, and that arbitration was the key to a successful strike resolution. When the Pullman strike occurred a month after the Great Northern strike, he had hopes for the same outcome.

Another figure who would play a role in the upcoming Pullman Strike was Illinois governor John Peter Altgeld. Although he was never a member of a union, Altgeld was sympathetic to workers. The son of poor German immigrants, he served as a Union soldier in the Civil War. After the war he moved west, working as a common laborer. He eventually became a teacher. Later he studied law and was elected district attorney for a Missouri county in 1874.

Altgeld moved to Chicago to practice law and, in 1884, wrote a small book on crime called *Our Penal Machinery and Its Victims*. In his book he said that the poor had a less than fair chance in American life because

John Altgeld, who served as the governor of Illinois from 1893 through 1897, was admired by labor supporters as one of the few politicians who consistently stood up for the rights of workers. (Illinois State Historical Library, Springfield)

crowded cities and low wages bred crime. Altgeld thought the courts were not concerned about the welfare of the young men who were filling the jails.

Altgeld was elected to the superior court of Cook County, for which he became the chief justice. Altgeld became so influential among Illinois Democrats they nominated him for governor of Illinois in 1892.

Altgeld won the election. After only a few weeks in office, he considered three appeals for clemency for convictions from the Haymarket Square riots in 1886. Eight men had been charged with the murder of one

This 1893 political cartoon depicts Governor Altgeld releasing the hounds of socialism, anarchy, and murder with his pardon of the surviving Haymarket defendants. The monument erected in memory of the Chicago police officers who were killed or wounded in the Haymarket Riot is pictured in the background. (Library of Congress)

THE FRIEND OF MAD DOGS.

Governor Altgeld of Illinois in freeing the Anarchists bitterly denounced Judge Gary and the Jury that convicted them.

officer, but only three of those were still alive. Five had been sentenced to death, though one of the prisoners had committed suicide the night before he was to be executed. Four others were hanged by the state the next day. Two of the remaining three—Samuel Fielden and Michael Schwab—had been sentenced to life in prison. Oscar Neebe was serving fifteen years.

Altgeld studied the facts of the trial carefully, and decided that the judge had been prejudiced and the jury had been packed with management sympathizers. Altgeld pardoned the three men and stated his belief that all eight had been innocent. Altgeld carefully described the evidence and his reasons for the pardons when they were issued, but many people disagreed. He was criticized and attacked in the newspapers, and would ultimately not be reelected.

Altgeld's experience with the Haymarket convictions made him determined to do what he thought was right even if it was not popular. He remained true to this decision when the Pullman Strike broke out a year later.

3.
A Company Town

Eugene Debs represented one side of the debate between workers and management that erupted during the Pullman Strike. He spoke for the workers who wanted a larger portion of the immense wealth they were helping to create in the post-Civil War industrial boom.

George Mortimer Pullman embodied the opposing side of the conflict. In many ways Pullman was an example of what had come to be called the American Dream—the idea that anyone who is hardworking, inventive, and farsighted can become a great success by participating in the dynamic American economy.

Born in 1831, Pullman was one of ten children of a skilled and hardworking but poor mechanic. He had to quit school at fourteen to work in a store but continued

to study by himself at night. One of his brothers taught him cabinetmaking. When the state of New York widened the Erie Canal, Pullman got a job there and learned about moving buildings and improving drainage.

In 1855, when young Pullman learned that Chicago needed men to raise streets and buildings on land being eroded by Lake Michigan, he traveled to that growing city. During the long train trip he could not sleep in the cramped, dirty bunk with its lumpy mattress, stuffy air, and constant jolting. He stopped trying to sleep, got up, sat at the end of the car, and thought about the possibilities for better sleeping accommodations on trains.

Excited about his ideas, Pullman took a position with the Woodruff Sleeping Car Company and helped convert two regular coaches into sleeping cars. With his cabinetry skills he was able to supervise the carpenters and worked with them to get exactly what he wanted.

Pullman expected great success from his sleeping car, but it did not come. Temporarily discouraged, he went off to Colorado during the gold rush. He returned to Chicago in 1864 and decided to try his sleeping car idea again. This time he had a different plan. He spent $20,000—instead of the usual $5,000—on a railroad sleeping car and constructed the Pioneer. The Pioneer was a day coach that turned into a sleeper at night, with upper berths on shelves that swung into the ceiling. Pullman was careful to make the car beautiful as well as comfortable.

Overleaf: *Pullman founder George Mortimer Pullman.* (Courtesy of Getty Images.)

George Pullman's precursor to the luxurious Pullman Car, the Pioneer.

The Pioneer was one foot wider and two-and-a-half feet taller than regular cars, so some railroads were not willing to try it at first. Then, in 1865, the Pioneer was used by the Chicago & Alton Railroad to transport the body of the assassinated President Lincoln to Springfield, Illinois. This helped popularize the new style of railroad passenger car.

In 1867, Pullman incorporated the Pullman Palace Car Company in Illinois. It began manufacturing dining cars, parlor cars, and private cars as well as sleepers. Pullman sold cars in the United States as well as England, Scotland, and Italy. By 1879, his manufacturing plant in Detroit and the repair units in three other cities were no longer sufficient to handle the increased business. Pullman needed more room and decided to build a new factory with a model town around it near Chicago, Illinois.

Pullman wanted to make life healthier and happier for his workers. He thought he could do so and make more money at the same time. He had read about three

An 1894 advertisement for Pullman car service. (Library of Congress)

PULLMAN PORTERS

Pullman cars were known across the country and easily recognizable because most were painted a dark "Pullman green." A Pullman ticket was expensive, but passengers were rewarded with luxurious surroundings. Each car was staffed by a porter, dressed in the company's signature white cotton coat, who was usually called "George" by passengers. He made up each passenger's bed at night, put it away in the morning, shined shoes, carried luggage, and generally made himself available to satisfy any request or demand. These porters were almost exclusively African American, and though they were rewarded with higher pay than they could have realized in other jobs available to them at the time, they worked extremely long hours—as much as four hundred a month. Pull-man porters often became leaders in the black com-munity, and their constant travel around the country put them in an excellent position to bring messages and news to the towns and neighborhoods in which they stayed while on the road. In 1925, despite fe-rocious opposition from the company, Pullman porters were organized into the first all-black union, the Broth-erhood of Sleeping Car Porters, by A. Philip Ran-dolph. He would go on to the lead the fight to bring African-American workers into American unions and help to jump-start the civil rights movement.

Pullman porter organizer and civil rights activist A. Philip Randolph. (Smithsonian Institution, Washington, DC)

experimental industrial towns in Europe that had suc-cess combining work and home: Saltaire, England; Guise, France; and Essen, Germany. Pullman may have visited Saltaire, where alpaca woolens were manufactured, when he was in England selling his cars. His town greatly resembled Saltaire.

George Pullman chose 4,000 acres on the prairie, twelve miles south of downtown Chicago. He sought the advice of architects, engineers, and industrial experts while building his town. But most of his advisors did not stay employed with Pullman for long. Although he had a remarkable memory and grasp of detail, his personality was brusque, and he was not easy to get along with.

Construction of the town of Pullman, named in honor of the founder, began in 1880. The factory shops were built first and, by April 1881, were rolling out railroad cars.

Pullman did not cut corners in building the town. He

This colorized photograph, taken when the plant was less than a decade old, shows the water tower and front entrance to the Pullman factory shops. (Library of Congress)

wanted only the best and most advanced features. Cream-colored clay for the bricks was taken from nearby Lake Calumet. An advanced sewer system allowed sewage to flow downhill to a reservoir, where it was pumped to a basin to be filtered through tiles. The clean water was drained into Lake Calumet, and the organic matter was used on a model farm that yielded an 8 percent profit from vegetables sold in the town and in Chicago. A dairy farm of one hundred cows was also included. There was a gas plant, and icehouses on the shores of Lake Calumet. Heat created in the shops' boilers was piped to warm the public buildings and the better-quality residences.

Pullman featured a central square with public buildings and an arcade for the Pullman headquarters and other businesses. The Florence Hotel was built with brick, in the Queen Anne style, trimmed in stone, and roofed with slate. The town school maintained high

The town of Pullman's elegant Florence Hotel. (Library of Congress)

standards, and the children of Pullman were guaranteed schooling from kindergarten through eighth grade. An evening school was added to provide high school courses, including mechanical drawing, bookkeeping, and secretarial skills. There was also a theater, a church, and a library. The library was seldom used because people had to pay a three-dollar annual fee. Unlike Andrew Carnegie, who built 2,800 free libraries, Pullman believed that people would only appreciate books if they had to pay to read them.

There were other symptoms of potential problems in Pullman. The church was not used until 1886 because the rent was too high. No other churches were allowed to be built, although fifteen religious denominations rented rooms or held services in towns nearby. Alcohol was banned because Pullman believed drinking was a bad habit. Though some of the houses Pullman built were of higher quality than the housing workers would have had access to elsewhere, the rents were also much higher. Pullman owned everything in the town, which meant residents had to shop at the company stores, and prices were strictly regulated. Because a person's rent, for example, was deducted directly from his paycheck, many workers never received the money they earned— it went straight back into Pullman's coffers.

George Pullman was perplexed and hurt when his town was criticized as feudal or paternalistic. This means that, as in the Middle Ages, one man owns the land and controls much in the lives of the people who live on it, collecting rent and fees that he alone sets. Pullman felt that since people chose to live in his town he could not be accused of controlling their lives.

Many of the workers saw things differently. They felt that if they did not live in Pullman, they would not keep their jobs. This made them bitter because rents were higher than for comparable housing in nearby towns. Pullman countered by pointing out that the town provided many services, like mowing the grass and repairing the buildings. He had trouble grasping the fact that others wanted to participate in the economy, just as he did, by owning and maintaining their own homes. This was a strange lack of understanding on the part of Pullman, a strong believer in free enterprise and private property. After a visit to Pullman in 1885, a reporter for the *New York Sun* concluded:

> [The workers] want to run the municipal government themselves, according to the ordinary American fashion. They secretly rebel because the Pullman Company continues its watch and authority over them after working hours. They declare they are bound hand and foot by a philanthropic monopoly.

In the same year, a professor of economics from Johns Hopkins University visited Pullman and came to a similar conclusion:

> Here is a population of eight thousand souls where not one single resident dare speak out openly his

opinion about the town which he lives in. One feels that one is mingling with a dependent, servile people. There is an abundance of grievances, but if there lives in Pullman one man who would give expression to them in print over his own name, diligent inquiry continued for ten days was not sufficient to find him.

The situation was, Professor Richard Ely concluded, "un-American," and created "the repression of all freedom." Such conditions could not last forever.

Labor trouble between Pullman and his employees would have a ripple effect throughout the industry. Pullman cars were used and serviced by many of the railroads—if Pullman workers went on strike, the work stoppage would affect them all.

In 1886, railroad owners had created an organization called the General Managers' Association, for "the consideration of problems of management arising from the operation of railroads terminating or centering in Chicago." There were twenty-four of these lines at that time, including such giant systems as the Illinois Central; the Baltimore & Ohio; the Chicago, Burlington & Quincy; the Chicago & Northwestern; the Chicago & Rock Island; and the Atchison, Topeka & Santa Fe. As the organization's name indicated, only managers could belong, and that meant only general managers, assistant general managers, and general superintendents. In 1894, the railroads represented by these managers had 41,000 miles of track, 221,000 workers, $818 million in capital stock, and over $102 million combined net annual earnings.

Working conditions and wages were the managers' major concerns. They pooled their information and shared it among themselves to help deal with demands for wage increases made by workers. They kept charts of what each railroad paid each type of worker, and each railroad would try to keep their salaries in line with the others in order to avoid having workers change jobs for higher pay. These pay rates were referred to as the "Chicago scale." Today, these actions would be called collusion, which is illegal.

For example, the general managers heard in February 1893 that there was a request coming to increase the wages of switchmen. The switchmen's union petitioned all of the railroads, because they knew about the Chicago scale and believed that no one railroad would increase wages unless they all did. The association quickly met and organized three committees to defeat the petition. They were determined to prove to the workers that they would not negotiate with unions.

The General Managers' Association was quick and efficient. The first committee, Committee No. 1, recruited and listed switchmen outside the region who would be willing to be brought in as temporary workers if the Chicago switchmen went on strike. Committee No. 2 was in charge of recording wage rates and making recommendations regarding increase requests. It surprised no one that Committee No. 2 recommended no increase for the switchmen. Committee No. 3 was to deal with city and county officials in case of a strike, informing them of anything illegal or violent that might justify police action. After finding out about this concerted defense, the switchmen wearily accepted defeat and voted not to strike.

Later that same month, baggage agents asked for a wage increase. Committee No. 2 approved an increase for baggage masters only; thus a few employees got raises while the rest got none. This action bred dissonance among the workers, which was exactly what the committee wanted. If the workers could be made to fight among themselves, they had less of a chance of organizing a unified front against the owners.

This combination of underpaid workers, higher rents, and management determined not to give in to the demands of organized labor created an environment seething with tensions and frustrations. But as long as there were jobs, the potential for a major strike only simmered; coming events would bring it to a boil.

4.
The Strike Spreads

One characteristic of this era was periodic financial panic, when people and lending institutions suddenly began hoarding their money because they feared an economic calamity was approaching. The unfortunate result was that the panic usually caused a depression. In 1893, a deep depression resulted from a series of panics. (It was considered to be the "Great Depression" until the more severe depression of the 1930s.) Millions of jobs were lost, and most of those who held onto their jobs had their wages cut.

At the beginning of the depression, Pullman workers were better off than most. The World's Columbian Exposition (also called the Chicago Fair) stimulated work at the Pullman Company because the 27 million visitors needed transportation. People who could afford to come to the exposition from long distances wanted the comfortable accommodations best provided by the Pullman Palace Cars.

THE CHICAGO FAIR

The World's Columbian Exposition was ostensibly held to commemorate the four hundredth anniversary of Christopher Columbus's arrival in America, but became a symbol of the advancements and achievements made in American society during the nineteenth century. Drawing more than 27 million visitors during the six months it was open (the population of the United States was just over 63 million), the fair was a showcase for the marvels and wonders of the new age. Celebrities and famous figures from all walks of life attended, from Jane Addams to Frederick Douglass to Nikola Tesla, whose revolutionary alternating current lit each of the fair's white-painted buildings at night, creating a glow that could be seen for miles.

This poster, inset with a portrait of President Grover Cleveland, was made to promote the opening of the 1893 World's Fair in Chicago. (Library of Congress)

After the exposition, however, the demand for new cars slowed. The Pullman Company did not need as many employees to build cars, although some were still needed to repair and refurbish cars already in service that were either rented or sold to railroads.

The business conditions of 1893-94 led directly to the Pullman Strike. Although George Pullman made an effort to avoid layoffs, he did cut wages. But most damaging was his refusal to lower rents and fees in his model town. The workers were desperate, caught in a trap of lower wages and higher rent and food costs. Because rent was taken directly from their paychecks, many

Company housing for the Pullman workers. (Library of Congress)

Pullman workers had only pennies left over with which to feed their families. One worker described his circumstances:

> My family consists of myself, wife and four children. We live in three small rooms with only a back entrance, for which I pay $9.00 per month, and fifty cents for water. I am considered a first-class car builder, and am a sober and industrious man and have always reported for work, whether day or piece work. I was worse off at the time of the strike by $250.00 than when I came to Pullman. In regard to wages of a '93, with strict economy we barely eked out an existence, but the first part of '94 new trouble began. The Company, not satisfied, began the war by reducing our wages to a starvation point. At the time we laid down our tools, we were building a car for $19.50 that we should have got $36 for. After the second cut in our wages the stores refused to give us credit, as they knew we could not pay in full from one pay day to another. More trouble began. The Company would not give us our checks at the shops as usual, but sent us to the Company's bank, where they would have a better chance to squeeze us for the rent it was impossible to pay. I have seen myself and fellow workmen pleading with the rent agent to leave us enough to buy some member of the family a pair of shoes or some other necessity. Then when our last cut came, that was the straw that broke the camel's back; we could not stand it any longer; I, like a good many

others, had to stop carrying my dinner, as what I
had to carry would have run through the basket. I
have seen one of my companions on the next car to
mine, so weak from the lack of proper food, that he
would have to rest on the way going home.

We could see plainly it was either work and starve,
or strike and depend on charity until we could win,
which we are bound to do. The good Lord is always
on the side of justice, and I am sure he will see
justice done us.

A few days after the strike began, Eugene Debs arrived in Pullman. He was unhappy about the Pullman
Strike because he did not think it came at a good time.
He knew that high levels of unemployment had created
a vast pool of workers desperate for jobs. The company
would have no trouble finding the replacement workers
that the strikers referred to as "scabs." But by May 16,
after he had spoken with many of the strikers, he felt they
had a legitimate complaint. Debs expressed his feelings:

> I believe a rich plunderer like Pullman is a greater
> felon than a poor thief, and it has become no small
> part of the duty of this organization to strip the mask
> of hypocrisy from the pretended philanthropist and
> show him to the world as an oppressor of labor. . . .
> The paternalism of Pullman is the same as the
> interest of a slave holder in his human chattels.

Reverend William Carwardine of the First Methodist Church of Pullman sided with the strikers and testified poignantly about their dilemma. He published a book about the strike and wrote about the relief organization that had been established to provide food for families suddenly without income. The first gift to the organization was from the mayor of Chicago's law firm in nearby Kensington. It contributed 25,000 pounds of flour and meat and the free use of a sick-care room. Other provisions followed, "from a bottle of ink to a car load of flour," said Carwardine, who also noted in his book that strikers and sympathizers wore white ribbons after a suggestion by Eugene Debs.

When Pullman Company supporters opposed to the strike pinned on American flags, some strike supporters added the flag to the top of their white ribbon in protest. "The American flag ought to be the best guaranty that an honest day's work should receive an honest day's pay," said Reverend F. Atchison, pastor of the Hyde Park Methodist Episcopal Church and a supporter of the strike.

The Pullman workers hoped they would receive formal support from the American Railway Union. Many of them were members. Its scheduled convention began in Chicago on June 12, 1894, just one month after the strike began. Many railway union members visited Pullman and talked with the strikers.

On June 21, a special committee of the American Railway Union, or ARU, proposed that if the Pullman

Jennie Curtis, president of ARU Local 269, was among those Pullman employees who addressed the American Railway convention. Her message was brief but poignant and is reproduced below.

Mr. President and Brothers of the American Railway Union:

We struck at Mr. Pullman because we were without hope. We joined the American Railway Union because it gave us a glimmer of hope. Twenty thousand souls, men, women, and little ones, have their eyes turned toward this convention today; straining eagerly through dark despondency for a glimmer of the heaven-sent message which you alone can give us on this earth.

Pullman, both the man and the town, is an ulcer on the body politic. He owns the houses, the schoolhouse, and the churches of God in the town he gave his once humble name.

And, thus, the merry war—the dance of skeletons bathed in human tears—goes on; and it will go on, brothers, forever unless you, the American Railway Union, stop it; end it; crush it out.

And so I say, come along with us, for decent conditions everywhere!

Company did not agree to arbitration by June 26, there should be a boycott on handling Pullman cars everywhere. The committee also called for employees of other Pullman factories to strike. The larger body of the union accepted the proposal. Pullman's vice president, Thomas Wickes, was informed of the union's demands.

The American Railway Union thought that the boycott would result in a loss of business, and that this economic pressure would force the Pullman Company to arbitrate with the strikers. The tactics were spelled out by Debs in this manner: car inspectors would refuse to inspect Pullman cars, switchmen would refuse to couple them onto trains, and engineers would refuse to move

This 1894 political cartoon, published on the cover of Harper's Weekly, *comments on Eugene Debs's involvement in the Pullman strike, showing a glum Debs perched on an impassable bridge entitled the "Highway of Trade." Behind him, the entire city has come to a stop.* (Courtesy of the Granger Collection.)

KING DEBS.

trains forward with Pullman cars on them. If these workers were fired and replaced, then all railroad workers
would immediately stop working in support.

On June 26, the boycott deadline, Pullman and Wickes
again said there was "nothing to arbitrate." By June 28,
about 18,000 workers were on strike. Major railroads,
including the Illinois Central, the Chicago & Northwestern, and the Atchison, Topeka & Santa Fe, were seriously
affected by the strike in Pullman.

After the intervention of the American Railway Union,
the general managers realized they were no longer deal-
ing with local brotherhoods of switchmen or brakemen,
but with a large umbrella organization. The managers
were furious that the railroads were being punished
when the Pullman Company only did business with
passenger railroads, and was not a railroad itself. They
thought it intolerable for workers to prevent the railroads from fulfilling their contracts because of a dispute
with Pullman. They voted to discharge any worker who
joined the strike and never to rehire him.

After this vote, Committee No. 1 began hiring replacement workers from outside the Chicago region and guar-
anteeing these new workers protection. This was easily
done by telegraphing other railroad managers, who then
ran ads in their cities. Soon there were thousands of
workers eagerly signing up for the new jobs.

Committee No. 3 set up an office, open twenty-four
hours a day, where any manager could report interference with train movements, violence, or the need for

police protection. The goal was to suggest there was an atmosphere of lawlessness that would prompt the government authorities to become involved on management's side. The office made frequent requests for intervention to the police, the sheriff, and eventually the United States marshal.

The general managers also asked for legal advice from the best railroad lawyers. These lawyers told them that for successful prosecution of offenders, the managers needed to find the best claims to convince federal authorities that they should intervene on management's side.

The most readily available actions that involved federal laws were accusations of interference with the U.S. mail and interstate commerce. These charges could be made through the U.S. district attorney's office. The general managers' chief strategy became to turn the struggle between workers and their employers into a battle between workers and the government. Following this strategy, they withdrew passenger trains from scheduled runs and said railroads would not accept freight since they could not guarantee being able to move it. This freight included U.S. mail.

On that same day, the general managers' antistrike manager, John Egan, announced that the American Railway Union had fought the railroads to a standstill. He said that only federal troops from Fort Sheridan, just north of Chicago, could restore law and quell the strike and boycott.

By July 2, the American Railway Union members realized their plan to bring the railroads to the bargaining table had been foiled, and that the general managers were actually trying to increase delays and inconvenience so the public would clamor for federal intervention. The union had made a mistake.

U.S. attorney general Richard Olney began receiving complaints about forcible seizures of trains by strikers and other incidents of violence. Square-faced, with stern eyes and a drooping mustache, Olney was known for taking prompt and forceful action. A former railroad lawyer, he was opposed to the workers going on strike. Olney, President Grover Cleveland, General John Schofield of the U.S. Army, and War Secretary Daniel Lamont kept tabs on the strike from Washington, DC. Olney encouraged Cleveland to issue orders to stop the strikers from interfering with the mail.

Debs explained that American Railway Union members were not stopping the mail. They simply wanted the railroads to remove Pullman cars from trains. The general managers argued that if trains ran without Pullman cars, the railroads would be guilty of breaking their contracts with the Pullman Company. Therefore, they could not allow the trains to leave without the Pullman cars. This meant the trains could not run, which resulted in a delay or standstill of the mail on some passenger trains.

The general managers' plan worked. This argument gave Olney the opening he needed to intervene in the

Attorney General Richard Olney would go on to become President Cleveland's secretary of state. (Library of Congress)

strike. On June 28, Olney issued telegrams to U.S. district attorneys instructing them to arrest any people obstructing mail trains. On June 30, Olney also authorized the swearing-in of deputies by the U.S. marshal. These deputies would ride the mail trains as guards.

On July 1, reports of disturbances in towns outside of Chicago were sent to Washington by both U.S. district attorney Thomas Milchrist and U.S. marshal J. W. Arnold. The next day, Olney ordered federal judges in Chicago to issue a restraining order, called an injunction, against Debs and the American Railway Union. This injunction forbade them to encourage, persuade, or threaten railroad workers to abandon their jobs. They were also forbidden to hinder "mail trains, express trains, or other trains, whether freight or passenger, engaged in interstate commerce." The federal government had moved to the side of Pullman and the general managers to end the strike.

In 1887, Congress had passed the Interstate Commerce Act. The purpose of the law had been to regulate the rates railroads could charge farmers and other manufacturers to transport their goods. It had been advocated for years by farmers and others who were forced to pay the railroads exorbitant fees. Now Olney used the Interstate Commerce Act to justify the action he took against the strikers because they were restricting trade. The Sherman Antitrust Act of 1890 was intended to slow the growth of trusts that were stamping out competition in many industries by setting prices instead of letting the free market system establish what a product or service was worth. Now Olney used the Sherman Antitrust Act to argue that the

INJUNCTIONS

An injunction is a court order that proscribes or prohibits an action. Injunctions are used most often in equity courts, which focus on righting wrongs through action, not reparation. For instance, the owner of a factory whose workers are striking might ask the court for an injunction, which would legally prevent workers from striking. In contrast, if he were to sue the workers for damages caused by the work stoppage, it is unlikely he would be able to recover the sum, or that his business would survive the wait. Injunctions have to be enforced to be effective, so a factory owner could ask the appropriate law enforcement officials to act on his behalf.

In 1932, the Federal Anti-Injunction Act restricted federal injunctions against workers. In 1947, the Taft-Hartley Act restored some injunction powers to the courts. In 1959, the Labor-Management Reporting and Disclosure Act allowed injunctions in order to promote higher ethical standards within unions. Injunctions have been used more recently in other areas, such as civil rights legislation. Injunctions, for example, have enforced racial desegregation of schools since the 1970s.

Below is the partial text of the injunction presented to Debs and the American Railway Union leaders, addressed to the defendants

and all persons combining and conspiring with them, and all other persons whomsoever, absolutely to desist and refrain from in any way or manner interfering with, hindering, obstructing, or stopping any of the business of any of the following named railroads . . . as common carriers of passengers and freight between or among any states of the United States, and from in any way or manner interfering with, hindering, obstructing, or stopping any mail trains, express trains, or other trains, whether freight or passenger, engaged in interstate commerce, or carrying passengers or freight between or among the states; and from in any manner interfering with, hindering, or stopping any trains carrying the mail; and from in any manner interfering with, hindering, obstructing, or stopping any engines, cars, or rolling stock of any of said companies engaged in interstate commerce, or in connection with the carriage of passengers or freight between or among the states; and from in any manner interfering with, injuring, or destroying any of the property of any of said railroads engaged in, or for the purpose of, or in connection with interstate commerce, or the carriage of the mails of the United States, or the transportation of passengers or freight between or among the states; and from entering upon the grounds or premises of any of said railroads for the purpose of interfering with, hindering, obstructing, or stopping any of said mail trains, passenger or freight trains engaged in interstate commerce, or in the transportation of passengers or freight between or among the states, or for the purpose of interfering with, injuring, or destroying any of said property so engaged in or used in connection with interstate commerce, or the transportation of passengers or property between or among the states; and from injuring or destroying any part of the tracks, roadbed, or road or permanent structures of said railroads; and from injuring, destroying, or in any way interfering with any of the signals or switches of any of said railroads; and from displacing or extinguishing any of the signals of any of said railroads; and from spiking, locking, or in any manner fastening any of the switches of any of said railroads; and from uncoupling or in any way hampering or obstructing the control by any of said railroads of any of the cars, engines, or parts of trains of any of said railroads engaged in interstate commerce or in the transportation of passengers or freight between or among the states, or engaged in carrying any of the mails of the United States; and from compelling or inducing, or attempting to compel or induce, by threats, intimidation, persuasion, force, or violence, any of the employees of any of said railroads to refuse or fail to perform any of their duties as employees of any of said railroads in connection with the interstate business or commerce of such railroads or the carriage of the United States mail by such railroads, or the transportation of passengers or property between or among the states; and from compelling or inducing, or attempting to compel or induce, by threats, intimidation, force, or violence any of the employees of any of said railroads who are employed by such railroads, and engaged in its service in the conduct of interstate business or in the operation of any of its trains carrying the mail of the United States, or doing interstate business, or the transportation of passengers and freight between and among the states, to leave the service of such railroad; and from preventing any person whatever, by threats, intimidation, force, or violence from entering the service of any of said railroads, and doing the work thereof, in the carrying of the mails of the United States or the transportation of passengers and freight between or among the states; and from doing any act whatever in furtherance of any conspiracy or combination to restrain either of said railroad companies or receivers in the free and unhindered control and handling of interstate commerce over the lines of said railroads, and of transportation of persons and freight between and among the states; and from ordering, directing, aiding, assisting, or abetting in any manner whatever any person or persons to commit any or either of the acts aforesaid.

American Railway Union and Pullman strikers had formed an illegal trust. Therefore, the government had the right to break up the strike as an illegal act. Ironically, two laws that were passed to control the power of giant business were now being used against the workers.

The injunction was personally presented to Debs and printed in newspapers and posted in public places for all to read. In the July 3 edition of the *New York Times,* the injunction was angrily called a "Gatling gun on paper" and "a veritable dragnet in matter of legal verbiage, one of these peculiar instruments that punishes an individual for doing a certain thing, and is equally

This 1894 illustration from an American newspaper depicts the police trying to quell a mob of rioting workers in order to allow a train to pass. (Courtesy of the Granger Collection.)

merciless if he does not do it," but most newspapers agreed with Olney's action.

When U.S. marshal Arnold went to the scene of a disturbance in the Rock Island rail yards at Blue Island near Chicago and read the injunction aloud, he was jeered by a crowd of 2,000 strike sympathizers. He telegraphed an alarming report to Olney of "a desperate time" and complained of his "inadequate force." Arnold also reported mobs detaching mail cars, overturning freight cars, and taking control of rail junctions. His judgment was that it would be "impossible to move trains here without having the Fifteenth Infantry from Fort Sheridan ordered here."

Arnold soon got what he wanted. President Cleveland told General Schofield to move troops to Chicago. The troops arrived after midnight and found the city quiet. No trains were moving. Although the Blue Island disturbance had been off in a remote southern suburb, the troops were sent not only to Blue Island but also to the Chicago Stock Yards. These troop movements were based upon the advice of Marshal Arnold, District Attorney Milchrist, and the general managers' representative John Egan.

Illinois governor John Altgeld was furious when he heard that federal troops were in Chicago. Neither Cleveland nor Olney had informed Altgeld that Army soldiers were coming. The U.S. Constitution requires that the state legislature or the governor must make requests for help in their own state. Federal officials are restricted from sending in troops for their own purposes. That President Cleveland had sent in troops without even advising Altgeld and without waiting for a request from Illinois authorities was a direct insult to the governor.

Governor Altgeld thought that the Chicago police, the Cook County sheriff, and the Illinois militia had the situation under control. He believed Chicago superintendent of police Michael Brennan, Mayor John Hopkins, and Cook County sheriff James Gilbert when they reported their forces had the situation in hand. Altgeld had already established a reputation for sending Illinois troops to areas of trouble when requested by sheriffs. In the Pullman Strike, he had responded to requests from the Cairo, Decatur, Danville, and Springfield sheriffs for assistance. There was no need for federal troops.

Altgeld suspected that John Egan and his general managers' Committee No. 3 were exaggerating incidents and the potential for danger to federal officials and pretending that they desperately needed help that local and state officials could not provide. While the railroad managers had reported disorders bordering on anarchy, investigating local police had found the disturbances to be considerably less violent than the managers had claimed.

Governor Altgeld telegraphed a protest to President Cleveland and Attorney General Olney. He said newspaper accounts of obstructive incidents "have in some cases been pure fabrications and in others wild exaggerations." Many trains were not moving because the railroads could not get men to operate them. The railroads were saying that mobs were causing the standstill in order to win public sympathy.

Governor Altgeld also stated his belief that Cleveland and Olney had violated the Constitution by sending in troops without his or the Illinois legislature's request:

> To absolutely ignore a local government in matters of this kind, when that government is ready to furnish any assistance needed, and is amply able to enforce the law, not only insults the people of the State ... but is in violation of a basic principle of our institutions. . . . Under our Constitution Federal supremacy and local self-government must go hand-

in-hand, and to ignore the latter is to do violence to the Constitution.

Altgeld requested that all U.S. troops be removed from Chicago. Cleveland replied that he had the legal right to protect the U.S. mail. In reply, Altgeld sent him a lengthy telegram protesting Cleveland's assumption of power. It was to no avail. Cleveland was not going to remove the troops.

The arrival of the troops seemed to feed the hoodlum element in the city. There were already many tramps and petty criminals who had come to Chicago for the Columbian Exposition and had become stranded by the depression of 1893. Restless, cunning, and now excited,

This painting, from a July 1894 photograph, shows federal troops encamped north of Illinois Central Railroad near downtown Chicago's Loop. (Illinois State Historical Library, Springfield)

they were like a dash of gasoline thrown on a fire. On the evening of July 4, these vagabonds were roaming train tracks in mobs that included teenage boys and even some women and children. The next day they were pushing over freight cars, setting a few on fire, throwing switches, and stoning trains.

On the night of July 5, a huge fire burned many buildings of the Columbian Exposition in Jackson Park. No suspects were arrested, but strike sympathizers were quickly blamed.

On July 6, another mob started fires in the Illinois Central yards by igniting freight cars. The wind was strong, and the flames spread down the lines of box cars where fire hoses could not reach. The belching red-and-black mass of destruction roared for several miles before it was stopped. That evening, seven hundred cars were also looted and torched in the Panhandle yards in South Chicago near Fiftieth Street. The Illinois militia was dispatched to clear the tracks and restore order.

The mobs continued their destruction on July 7. At the intersection of Loomis and Forty-ninth Streets, a moving train stopped for crew and soldiers to clear an obstruction on the tracks. A nearby mob of several thousand hurled stones at the crew and soldiers. The troop commander ordered a bayonet charge that injured several people. This attack further angered the mob. They overturned a flat car, threw more stones, and even fired bullets. After four soldiers were wounded, the

Flames engulf hundreds of freight cars in the Illinois Central yards during the riots on the night of July 6. (Courtesy of the North Wind Picture Archives.)

commander ordered his men to fire into the crowd. This action finally dispersed the mob, but not before four rioters were killed and twenty wounded. This was the climax of the riot in Chicago.

The malicious destruction by lawless rioters dissolved whatever sympathy most people had for the Pullman strike and boycott, although Pullman employees were not among the roving mobs. The Pullman workers had even taken precautions to avoid violence at the onset of the strike by establishing protective guards at the Pullman plant. But they were still blamed for the violence, along with boycotting members of the American Railway Union.

Newspapers everywhere were filled with the sensational details. Although some reporters wrote of union members trying to persuade the rioters to go home, most of the accounts were filled with lurid descriptions of violence.

Every Chicago resident was increasingly affected by the strike. The city was dependent on shipments of fruit, vegetables, milk, and meat. Thirteen railroads had ceased all movement by July 5, and ten were able to operate only passenger trains. This was not because of the rioters but because the railroad workers were enacting the boycott they had voted on.

The general managers knew it was time to make a move to kill the strike. On July 7, they proposed that the Chicago police, the Illinois militia, and the federal troops—more than 10,000 men altogether—coordinate their efforts. Mayor Hopkins agreed but said that no one commander could order the other organization's troops. The general managers brought in outside trainmen to run the trains under guard.

President Cleveland received many telegrams and letters from the people of Chicago who wanted to restore law and order and to return to business as usual. On July 8, Cleveland issued an executive proclamation warning the Chicago mobs to stop the violence and go home before noon on July 9. If they did not obey this proclamation, they would be treated as public enemies by soldiers.

July 10, 1894, marked the end of the Pullman Strike when a meat train, escorted by the U.S. Cavalry, left the Chicago stockyards. (Library of Congress)

The rioting in Chicago finally ended. Five people had been killed by the Illinois militia, none by federal troops. Sixteen had been seriously injured. The railroads had suffered several hundred thousand dollars in damage. Not a single Pullman car was destroyed because none were in the freight yards where the rioting broke out.

On July 10, the track from the Chicago Stock Yards was cleared, and the Rock Island railroad also resumed operation of suburban passenger trains. By July 13, everything was back to normal. On July 19, the federal troops were removed. The Illinois militia left gradually and was gone by August 7.

5.
A Chain Reaction

When the American Railway Union members voted on June 21, 1894, to boycott the handling of Pullman cars, they started a chain reaction. Soon workers in other Western states began boycotting and striking as well. In St. Louis, workers on the Missouri Pacific filed notice that they would not handle Pullman cars. When a switchman then refused to move a Pullman, he was fired. His co-union members requested his rehiring. When the request was rejected, all union members went out on strike.

There were also cases in which workers removed Pullman cars from the line but railroad managers refused to let trains leave. The Atchison, Topeka & Santa Fe Railroad was in serious financial trouble. Wages were several months overdue. This had already created tension among the workers, and the men showed their frustration by sidetracking Pullman cars. On July 1, in Trinidad, Colorado, a mob disarmed deputy marshals sent in to keep the peace.

> **The complaints brought by Pullman workers were not all that unusual for the time. Below is testimony given to the United States Strike Commission by former Pullman employee Theodore Rhodie, outlining the world in which he and his family lived.**
>
> August 16, 1894, Theodore Rhodie, being first duly sworn, testified as follows:
>
> 1. (Commissioner Wright): State your name, age, residence, and occupation.
>
> Ans. Theodore Rhodie, 39, live at No. 367 Stephenson Street, Pullman, Ill., am a painter.
>
> 2. (Commissioner Wright): Have you been employed at Pullman in the works there?
>
> Ans. Yes, sir.
>
> 3. (Commissioner Wright): How long have you been employed there?
>
> Ans. About twelve years.
>
> 4. (Commissioner Wright): As a painter?
>
> Ans. Yes, sir.
>
> 5. (Commissioner Wright): Are you a member of the American Railway Union?

Ans. Yes, sir.

6. (Commissioner Wright): How long have you been a member of that order?

Ans. Since April last, the 19th day of April, I think.

7. (Commissioner Wright): Are you one of the strikers at Pullman?

Ans. Yes, sir.

8. (Commissioner Wright): State what led you to strike, the cause, etc., in your own way?

Ans. About four years ago I had a job and there was another class of work they wanted me to do that nobody else could make a day's wages out of on piecework, and they wanted me to work in partnership with two or there or four other men, as many as might be necessary, to carry on that class of work, and whatever we made we were to divide equally, and I was to kind of oversee the work, that it was done properly and got out at the right time. I told them I would take the job under consideration and would see if I could get along with it, but if I could not make wages at it I would want my old place back. After they got me at it once I told them several times I did not like the job and would like to have my old place back, but I could not get it back; I was told I had to stay there or else get out. We get so after working a number of years at a certain class of work that we can make from $2.65 to $2.80 per day, working 10 3/4 hours per day; for work that I got $9 per hundred last fall I only got $4.25 at the time we struck. They kept cutting me down from last fall on the same kind of work and on the same amount of work we could not make $1.25 per day out of it; I told the foreman it was impossible to make anything at it, and he said if I didn't like it I could quit. There are also many other things which led us to strike—the abuse, and I owe them for rent and I [could] not pay [it], and I was in debt to my grocery man, to my butcher, and so on all along the line, and it was impossible for any of us to make a living.

9. (Commissioner Kernan): When you used the [word] abuse, what did you mean?

Ans. From the abuse the foreman gave us. They would talk to the men as though they were dogs. For instance, one time the foreman came up to me—he was looking after some sash—and he said he understood there should no more sash come up. I told him if that was the case he should give the men in the cabinet shop an order not to send any up; that I had nothing to do with it; that I could not interfere with another man's business; that I was only to attend to my own department. He said, "Why don't you fix it?" I said, "I can not fix it." He said, "Why can't you paint it up?" I said, "I can not do it and make a good job out of it." Then he said, "You had better ask somebody that can." I said, "Well, I will ask you. I have worked at this business now for twelve years, and I try to do the best I can, and will leave it to my foreman here whether I am doing my work as good as it can be done, or if they have anybody else here that can do it any better." He said, "If you can not do any better work than that you will have to quit," and said he was going to get somebody from St. Louis. Finally, he got a man from St. Louis and put him at it, but after it was done and went in the cars it was brought back, and I had to fix it up. The man from St. Louis did not do it as good as I did. I had to fix it over, and when I asked for pay for doing it the answer was, "Oh, we have a contract. You understood we were to see that the work was done right, and because you did not do it right was the reason you had to do it over again."

10. (Commissioner Kernan): Didn't you get any pay for the time . . . spent fixing it over?

Ans. No, sir; these men experiment a good deal at our expense. For instance, they will buy new material without knowing anything about how it is going to work up, and if the work turns out bad the workmen have to turn right around and fix it up so as to make it go out, and if they ask for extra pay they will not give it; lots of times they get English varnish in there which can not be [used] in the shops only when the atmosphere strikes it just right; if the air is a little damp, the varnish goes back on us, and of course, it then [causes] a great deal of unnecessary work which should not be done. We have to do the job over again, sometimes two or three times, and get nothing for it. If you ask the management to pay you for the time, they say, no, they can not do that; but they can ask you to do the work for nothing, and if you don't like to do it you can quit.

11. (Commissioner Wright): Do you live in one of the Pullman houses?

Ans. Yes, sir.

12. (Commissioner Wright): What rent do you pay?

Ans. Fifteen dollars rent and 71 cents for water.

13. (Commissioner Wright): How many rooms and what other accommodations do you have?

Ans. I have five rooms, part of a cellar, and part of a back yard.

14. (Commissioner Wright): How does the price you pay compare with the rent of similar houses with similar accommodations [in] adjoining localities?

Ans. You could get the same accommodations, I believe, at from $7 to $8 per month.

15. (Commissioner Wright): How large a lot of land belongs to your house?

Ans. I should say the frontage of those houses is from 16 to 20 feet.

16. (Commissioner Wright): How deep?

Ans. Thirty to 35 feet; that is, the house; the lot is deeper; I could not say just how deep.

17. (Commissioner Wright): Were you a member of any of the committees which attempted to secure a settlement of the difficulties at Pullman?

Ans. Yes, sir.

18. (Commissioner Wright): State what your experience was with reference to those efforts.

Ans. We sent a committee up to the management and they said they could do nothing for us.

19. (Commissioner Kernan): Were you on any of them?

Ans. No, sir.

20. (Commissioner Wright): I thought you said you were on a committee—we only want what you know of your own knowledge.

Ans. Well, I had nothing whatever to do with that part of it; I only know we sent committees there and they brought back reports.

21. (Commissioner Worthington): About how much did you earn in the month of April, 1894?

Ans. I could hardly tell that, but I know I did not have much left after my rent was taken out.

22. (Commissioner Worthington): About how much did you have after paying your rent?

Ans. From $12 to $15 every two weeks.

23. (Commissioner Worthington): Are you a man of family?

Ans. Yes, sir.

24. (Commissioner Wright): How long since you have paid any rent?

Ans. I believe I owed $2 or $3 for back rent before we went on the strike and I have not paid any since that.

25. (Commissioner Wright): Has there been any effort to collect any rent out of the tenants?

Ans. There was day before yesterday, I believe.

26. (Commissioner Wright): What form did that effort take?

Ans. I was not home, but they asked my wife if I was going to pay any rent; my wife told them that I would pay rent as soon as I could get work and earn enough to pay it; that I had no work and had no money, but would pay the rent as soon as I could get money enough to pay it.

27. (Commissioner Worthington): The Pullman shops are running now, are they not?

Ans. Yes, sir.

28. (Commissioner Worthington): Do you know what wages they are paying?

Ans. Only from hearsay; I hear they are paying some men from $2.50 to $3 per day, and other from $3 to $5.

29. (Commissioner Worthington): Have you made application to work since the strike?

Ans. No, sir.

30. (Commissioner Worthington): Is there any reason why you have not made application?

Ans. There is one reason, and that is, I do not like to walk up there and hand up my membership in the American Railway Union; because when a man asks me to give up my principles, my right as an American citizen, he might just as well ask me for my life.

31. (Commissioner Wright): Would you be expected to sever your connection with the union if you went to work at Pullman now?

Ans. Yes, sir.

32. (Commissioner Wright): Do you know that to be a condition of reentering the works?

Ans. Yes; I know that to be a fact. I know some [men] who went there, and after they had taken their card away from them and sent them to the foreman, the foreman said that he had nothing for them to do and did not want them, and did not give them their cards back again.

(Commissioner Wright): The witness, Rhodie, is subject to cross examination if anybody wishes to cross-examine him.

(No response. Witness excused.)

The American Railway Union knew the tensions created by the workers' refusals to move Pullman cars and the railroads' subsequent refusals to move trains without the cars attached could easily erupt into violence. On July 4, in an effort to forestall this, the union applied for a federal injunction to force the Union Pacific to operate trains without Pullman cars. The injunction was denied.

After receiving news of the problems in Colorado, President Cleveland ordered federal troops from Fort Logan, near Denver, to mobilize. After pausing to fix cut telegraph wires in Pueblo, the soldiers arrived in Trinidad on July 4. Forty-eight men were arrested and sent to Denver to be tried for contempt of court.

At Raton, New Mexico, when a strike ensued, passengers on disconnected Pullman cars were stranded in the yards with nowhere to go. The station manager found money to buy meals for them. Meanwhile, three hundred local coal miners came to Raton in sympathy with the strikers. The local sheriff warned the federal marshal that there would be real trouble if he tried to impose his will on the workers.

On the night of July 3, rioters in Raton released the brakes on sixteen boxcars. The cars roared down a steep grade, crashed into the yards, and blocked access. The next evening, against the sheriff's advice, federal troops arrived and the miners vanished. The strikers in Raton returned to work.

In California, both the general public and the majority of newspapers supported the strike and the boycott. For them, the Southern Pacific Railroad was a monopoly of giant proportions, not only controlling freight rates but spreading into ship lines, harbor connections, and even streetcars. Californians could not understand why the Sherman Antitrust Act was not applied to the Southern Pacific, while it was used against the Pullman strikers and American Railway Union boycotters.

The pro-strike sympathy was so strong that in some places marshals had trouble finding men to restore order. Some state militiamen said they would not charge or fire at crowds of civilians. In Los Angeles, the boycott proceeded peacefully and effectively, with no trains moving.

Sacramento was the hottest center of pro-union workers. Three-fourths of the 2,500 railroad workers there went on strike, and they were joined by another five hundred workers from surrounding towns. When the U.S. marshal ordered a mail train made up, the workers disconnected the Pullman cars.

These workers resisted when the deputies tried to arrest them. Frightened, the marshal wired the governor for state troops. When the troops arrived, some of them refused to charge or fire upon the strikers. Most of the troops also lived in California. Their reluctance to punish the strikers shows how angry the people of California were about the Southern Pacific monopoly in their state.

Now President Cleveland and Attorney General Olney decided that federal troops were necessary not only to

A train on the Central Pacific Railroad stops at a depot outside of Sacramento, California, where much of the West Coast support for the Pullman workers was based. (Library of Congress)

protect the mails and interstate commerce but also to keep the railroads open for the military. The rationale for this decision was based upon the fact that the government had helped finance the construction of the Central Pacific Railroad (now owned by the Southern Pacific) in the 1860s. Part of the railroad's obligation, in return for the federal financial assistance, was to carry U.S. troops when necessary for defense. This was such a time, according to Cleveland and Olney, which meant they could order in more force in the name of national security.

On July 11, five hundred Army soldiers came up the Sacramento River by boat. The next day they drove away crowds in the railroad yards without firing a shot. Several soldiers were killed, though, when a train they were guarding en route to San Francisco was derailed by sabotage. One striker was later killed in the Sacramento yards when soldiers fired upon a crowd that was pelting them with stones.

By July 13, the Central Pacific line from Ogden to San Francisco was in operation. Although trouble had been anticipated in Oakland, where women were rolling bandages and a temporary hospital had been organized, no violence occurred.

In Nebraska, Wyoming, and Utah, there was much sympathy for the strikers. In Wyoming, where the population along the railroad was largely railroad workers, there were few people who would not benefit from a successful strike. In Rawlins, Wyoming, the U.S. marshal and his deputies were ordered to leave town, but when the federal troops arrived to guard the trains, there was no resistance. By July 16, trains were moving from Omaha to San Francisco.

Running from St. Paul, Minnesota, to Seattle, Washington, the Northern Pacific was another railroad that had been built with government loans. It had agreed to transport both military and mail. On June 26, American Railway Union members had begun boycotting it. The action soon spread, accompanied by some vandalism, including the burning of a bridge.

On July 3, the Army commander of the Dakotas wired that he had received no mail since June 25. Attorney General Olney ordered troops to accompany trains along the entire Northern Pacific route. Along the way, the first trains witnessed angry but nonviolent demonstrations from strikers.

An 1890s route map shows the extensive network of stops on the Northern Pacific Railroad.

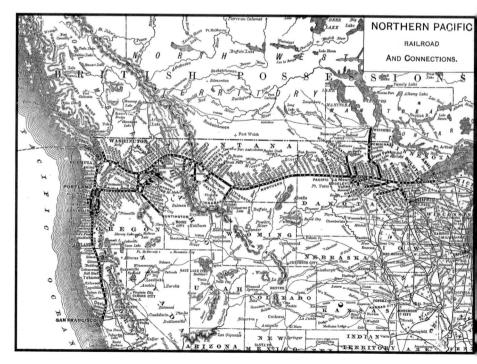

THE UNITED STATES POSTAL SERVICE

Organized in 1775 by the Second Continental Congress, what was then called the Post Office Department and is today the United States Postal Service is the second oldest federal agency in the country. Charged with carrying mail across the country, the postal service has tried just about every method imaginable. Mail has been moved by land, air, and sea. In the 1860s, mail was brought across the country by the famous Pony Express. In the 1950s, the post office even experimented with sending mail in a guided missile. Perhaps the most unusual postal

carrier was Dorsey, a dog who carried mail in California in the 1880s. Today, in Arizona, mules are used to bring mail to people living in the Grand Canyon.

Because the postal service is a department of the U.S. government, anyone interfering with its delivery is subject to prosecution under federal law, and federal troops can be used to ensure the mail is not interfered or tampered with.

Benjamin Franklin was the country's first postmaster general. (Library of Congress)

Oklahoma, though not yet a state in 1894, witnessed violence against the Rock Island Railroad. Trains were derailed and one bridge was blown up as a train passed over it. Marshals and deputies proved ineffective, and the governor called for federal troops on July 12.

In Iowa, particularly Sioux City and Dubuque, the governor called out the state militia after switches were thrown at junctions to halt trains.

From the east coming to Chicago, trains had to follow the southern coast of Lake Michigan through the city of Hammond, Indiana. Hammond sat at the junction of many railroads that employed members of the American Railway Union. These members were actively boycotting. They stopped trains and uncoupled the Pullman cars as they passed through to Chicago. But the governor of Indiana did not want state troops sent in because the boycott was being conducted peacefully.

When the U.S. marshal arrested some union officials in Hammond, the mood changed. Large mobs formed, with "recruits" drawn from the ranks of the hooligans and rioters of Chicago. These mobs created chaos by attacking replacement trainmen, derailing engines and cars, and taking over a Western Union telegraph office. By July 7, train traffic had completely stopped.

Though advised by his district attorney to call for federal troops, Governor Mathews of Indiana acted similarly to Governor Altgeld of Illinois. He stuck by his original decision and insisted the Indiana militia could handle the rioters.

Dismayed, Olney ordered in federal troops anyway. Some of these men, moving up and down the tracks, fired at anything even slightly suspicious. They killed a carpenter who was looking for his lost son, which created further resentment in Hammond because the carpenter was well known and liked.

The boycott did not move further east of Hammond, despite rallies of support in cities like Boston and New

York. There were few members of the American Railway Union in the East, where Wagner and Monarch sleeping cars were primarily used instead of Pullman cars.

But people there felt the effects nevertheless. According to New York newspapers, food prices soared for whatever goods were shipped in from the West. A box of peaches that usually cost one dollar shot to $3.60 on July 5. Chicken went up five cents a pound during the strike.

Another reason the boycott failed to move to the East was that the individual railway brotherhoods mistrusted and feared the American Railway Union. They did not want to become part of a large industrial union. They wanted to bargain in smaller groups as locomotive engineers, firemen, switchmen, trainmen, or conductors. A sympathetic strike was preposterous to them. Some eastern railroad workers even agreed with the general managers' argument that the railroads had made contracts with the Pullman Company and should not let the trains move without those Pullman cars on them.

The lack of sympathy was also created by greater unemployment among eastern railroad workers. About one-third of them were out of work. The depression of 1893 had taken a terrible toll. Many men in the East were eager to get work, and many were willing to replace strikers.

6.
Debs Goes to Jail

Despite the setback caused by the federal intervention on the side of the general managers, Eugene Debs continued to think the strikers and boycotters would win. The strikers' cause was also weakened when some of the Pullman plants did not join the strike. Pullman repair shops in Wilmington, Delaware, had refused unionization and never ceased operation. The repair shops in Ludlow, Kentucky, and St. Louis, Missouri, that had struck on June 25 were kept in operation with replacement workers.

Debs, always optimistic, was heartened by all the shutdowns in the West, even as the injunction and troop orders were carried out. His July 16 telegram still resounded with hopes of victory:

We have assurance that within 48 hours every labor organization will come to our rescue. The tide is on and the men are acquitting themselves like heroes. Here and there one weakens, but our cause is strengthened by others going out in their places.

But by July 18, the Pullman Company posted notice that the Chicago-area plant would reopen. Strikers could reapply for their jobs and would be hired only if they renounced their membership in the American Railway Union. The workers also had to accept their old wages and house rental rates in the town of Pullman.

PLEAS FROM THE GOVERNOR

The people of Pullman suffered greatly during and after the strike of 1894. Even those hired back to work at the company had trouble feeding their families, and those who remained out of work faced the prospect of starvation. Below are four letters written in the aftermath of the strike—one from a citizens' committee to Governor Altgeld and three increasingly agitated letters from the governor to George Pullman. Pullman's stance was as unequivocal as ever. He showed little sympathy for those suffering, saying only that they should not have gone on strike in the first place. Private citizens stepped in when Pullman did not, providing food and supplies to desperate residents. Eventually, many residents of Pullman moved away in hopes of finding better lives elsewhere. Today, the town of Pullman still stands, as part of the city of Chicago.

Kensington, Ill.,
August 17, 1894.

To His Excellency, the Governor of the State of Illinois:
We, the people of Pullman, who, by the greed and oppression of

George M. Pullman, have been brought to a condition where starvation stares us in the face, do hereby appeal to you for aid in this our hour of need. We have been refused employment and have no means of leaving this vicinity, and our families are starving. Our places have been filled with workmen from all over the United States, brought here by the Pullman Company, and the surplus were turned away to walk the streets and starve also. There are over 1600 families here in destitution and want, and their condition is pitiful. We have exhausted all the means at our command to feed them, and we now make this appeal to you as a last resource. Trusting that God will influence you in our behalf and that you will give this your prompt attention, we remain,

Yours in distress,
THE STARVING CITIZENS OF PULLMAN
F. E. POLLANS,
L. J. NEWELL,
THEO. RODHE,
Committee.

August 19, 1894.

To George M. Pullman, President Pullman Palace Car Co., Chicago:
Sir:—I have received numerous reports to the effect that there is great distress at Pullman. To-day I received a formal appeal as Governor from a committee of the Pullman people for aid. They state that sixteen hundred families including women and children, are starving; that they cannot get work and have not the means to go elsewhere; that your company has brought men from all over the United States to fill their places. Now these people live in your town and were your employees. Some of them worked for your company for many years. They must be people of industry and character or you would not have kept them. Many of them have practically given their lives to you. It is claimed they struck because after years of toil their loaves were so reduced that their children went hungry. Assuming that they were wrong and foolish, they had yet served you long and well and you must feel some interest in them. They do not stand on the same footing with you, so

that much must be overlooked. The State of Illinois has not the least desire to meddle in the affairs of your company, but it cannot allow a whole community within its borders to perish of hunger. The local overseer of the poor has been appealed to, but there is a limit to what he can do. I cannot help them very much at present. So unless relief comes from some other source I shall either have to call an extra session of the Legislature to make special appropriations, or else issue an appeal to the humane people of the State to give bread to your recent employees. It seems to me that you would prefer to relieve the situation yourself, especially as it has just cost the State upwards of fifty thousand dollars to protect your property, and both the State and the public have suffered enormous loss and expense on account of disturbances that grew out of trouble between your company and its workmen. I am going to Chicago to-night to make a personal investigation before taking any official action. I will be at my office in the Unity block at 10 a.m. to-morrow, and shall be glad to hear from you if you care to make any reply.

JOHN P. ALTGELD, Governor.

August 21st 1894.
Mr. George M. Pullman, President Pullman Car Company, Chicago, Ill.:
Sir:—I have examined the conditions at Pullman yesterday, visited even the kitchens and bedrooms of many of the people. Two representatives of your company were with me and we found the distress as great as it was represented. The men are hungry and the women and children are actually suffering. They have been living on charity for a number of months and it is exhausted. Men who had worked for your company for more than ten years had to apply to the relief society in two weeks after the work stopped.

I learn from your manager that last spring there were 3,260 people on the pay roll; yesterday there were 2,200 at work, but over 600 of these are new men, so that only about 1,600 of the old employees have been taken back, thus leaving over 1,600 of the old employees who have not been taken back, a few hundred have left, the remainder have nearly all applied for work, but were told that they were not needed. These are utterly destitute. The relief committee on last Saturday gave out two pounds of oat meal and two pounds of corn meal to each family. But even the relief committee has exhausted its resources.

Something must be done at once. The case differs from instances of destitution found elsewhere, for generally there is somebody in the neighborhood able to give relief; this is not the case at Pullman. Even those who have gone to work are so exhausted that they cannot help their neighbors if they would. I repeat now that it seems to me your company cannot afford to have me appeal to the charity and humanity of the State to save the lives of your old employees. Four-fifths of those people are women and children. No matter what caused this distress, it must be met.

If you will allow me, I will make this suggestion: If you had shut down your works last fall when you say business was poor, you would not have expected to get any rent for your tenements. Now, while a dollar is a large sum to each of these people, all the rent now due you is a comparatively small matter to you. If you would cancel all rent to October 1st, you would be as well off as if you had shut down. This would enable those who are at work to meet their most pressing wants. Then if you cannot give work to all why work some half-time so that all can at least get something to eat for their families. This will give immediate relief to the whole situation. And then by degrees assist as many to go elsewhere as desire to do so, and all to whom you cannot give work. In this way something like a normal condition could be re-established at Pullman before winter and you would not be out any more than you would have been had you shut down a year ago.

I will be at the Unity block for several hours and will be glad to see you if you care to make any reply.

Yours, respectfully,
JOHN P. ALTGELD.

Chicago, August 21st, 1894.

George M. Pullman, Esq., President Pullman Palace Car Company, City.

Sir:—I have your answer to my communication of this morning. I see by it that your company refuses to do anything toward relieving the situation at Pullman. It is true that Mr. Wickes offered to take me to Pullman and show me around. I told him that I had no objections to his going, but that I doubted the wisdom of my going under anybody's wing. I was, however, met at the depot by two of your representatives, both able men, who accompanied me everywhere. I took pains to have them present in each case. I also called at your office and got what information they could give me there, so that your company was represented and heard, and no man there questioned either the condition [or] the extent of the suffering. If you will make the round I made, go into the houses of the people, meet them face to face and talk with them, you will be convinced that none of them had $1,300, or any other [sum] of money only a few weeks ago.

I cannot enter into a discussion with you as to the merits of the controversy between you and your former workmen.

It is not my business to fix the moral responsibility in this case. There are nearly six thousand people suffering for the want of food—they were your employees—four-fifths of them women and children—some of these people have worked for you for more than twelve years. I assumed that even if they were wrong and had been foolish, you would not be willing to see them perish. I also assumed that as the State had just been to a large expense to protect your property you would not want to have the public shoulder the burden of relieving distress in your town.

As you refuse to do anything to relieve suffering in this case, I am compelled to appeal to the humanity of the people of Illinois to do so.

Respectfully yours,
JOHN P. ALTGELD

Debs had been consulting with constitutional lawyers in Chicago during the strike and was convinced that he was acting within the law as long as he did not advocate violence, which he hated. However, while Debs abhorred physical violence, he believed property damaged was an acceptable casualty. Because of the violence—both to people and to property—that had occurred, U.S. district attorney Thomas Milchrist in Chicago decided to arrest Debs. Attorney General Olney in Washington agreed with this decision.

During the second week of July, a grand jury in Chicago was ordered to examine evidence against Eugene Debs. If it found sufficient evidence that Debs had violated the July 2 injunction, then he would be arrested and tried for conspiracy to disrupt the mail.

The jury was given copies of some of Debs's telegrams, which had been subpoenaed from Western Union. No calls to violence were found, but his urgings to support the boycott seemed to indicate conspiracy, defined by Judge Peter Grosscup as "an agreement on the part of two or more individuals to stop trains unlawfully [that] would have the effect of halting mail trains and interstate commerce."

On July 10, Debs and three American Railway Union officers were indicted by the grand jury and arrested for the first time. They were charged with conspiracy to obstruct the U.S. mail. It took several hours to raise the bail of $10,000. After paying bail, each was allowed to go free until the trial began seven days later.

On July 17, Debs and his colleagues were arrested on

Eugene Debs, not long after his contempt trial. (Library of Congress)

a second charge: being in contempt of the court's July 2 injunction by multiple and willful violations. This time Debs refused to pay the bail money. He explained, "The poor striker who is arrested would be thrown in jail. We are no better than he."

The hearing began on July 23. Debs's lawyers argued that the contempt charges and the conspiracy charges were for the same actions. Because it is illegal to try a person twice for the same offense, they argued to have the contempt charge dropped.

After the judge ruled in disagreement, Debs's lawyers asked for a jury trial in a criminal court. They felt that a decision in an equity court by a judge would only be prejudiced against Debs and the American Railway Union. This request was also denied.

In the contempt trial that followed, the prosecuting lawyers argued that the government has the right to remove a "public nuisance." They claimed that a railroad was one kind of a public highway, and since courts could remove obstacles on roads, they could do the same on rails. By uniting workers to withdraw service from an interstate railroad, the union leaders had obstructed travel flow. According to this reasoning, the workers and Debs were guilty of being a public nuisance and were thus in contempt of the injunction.

On December 14, the judge declared Debs and his codefendants guilty of contempt. Debs was sentenced to six months in prison, the three other men to three months each. They began serving their sentences on January 8, 1895, in the Woodstock jail because the Cook County jail in Chicago was full.

Debs's lawyers appealed to the United States Supreme Court. They argued that the contempt trial had been conducted in the wrong court and was therefore unconstitutional. They further argued that refusal to work for a railroad is not a crime and that the interference with interstate commerce and mail delivery was incidental to the strike, not directly intended by it. Finally, they said that to be charged for a crime, defendants have the right to be tried in a criminal court and receive a trial by jury. The lawyers pointed out that Debs and his men had not received these rights in their equity court trial by a judge.

Attorney General Richard Olney argued against Debs before the Supreme Court. He said the union officials were no more blameless than a man holding a lighted match near gunpowder. Olney went on to say that the government is like a trustee, and it must protect the property that is committed to its care.

On May 27, 1895, the Supreme Court unanimously agreed with Olney. This decision, which came to be known as the Debs Decision or *In re Debs,* Latin for "about the Debs matter," established an important principle for strong federal power. The Supreme Court's decision stated that the federal government has the power to prevent interference with the mail and interstate commerce because the Constitution gives that same federal government the power to control the postal system and to make laws regarding interstate commerce. It also decided that a court of equity may be used by the government to rule about public nuisances, because the federal government has the constitutional power to remove obstructions to interstate commerce and the U.S. mails. "If emergency arises," the Court said, "the army of the Nation, and all its militia, are at the service of the Nation to compel obedience to its laws." The injunction did not forbid the workers to quit work; its purpose had been to remove obstructions from the rails on which interstate commerce and the mails traveled. The court concluded:

> The entire strength of the nation may be used to enforce in any part of the land the full and free exercise of all national powers and the security of all rights entrusted by the Constitution to its care. The strong arm of the national government may be put forth to brush away all obstructions to the freedom of interstate commerce or the transportation of mails.

Having been sentenced for contempt and having lost his appeal to the Supreme Court, Debs was next tried for conspiracy, along with twenty other American Railway Union officials. This trial was heard by a jury in a criminal court with Judge Grosscup presiding. It began on January 24, 1895. Debs was brought in every day from the Woodstock jail fifty miles away.

The defendants denied that they had entered into a conspiracy to paralyze the railroads. They claimed they were not in conspiracy against the injunction because they had advised workers to peacefully and lawfully stop work. Their actions had been motivated only by grievances with the Pullman Company and the railroads that carried Pullman cars. In fact, they insisted the railroads and the Pullman Company were partnered in a conspiracy to reduce wages and prevent the American

Railway Union members from receiving arbitration. Lawyers Clarence Darrow and Stephen Strong Gregory defended Debs. Darrow began the defense by charging that the prosecuting attorney was a "puppet in the hands of the great railroad corporations in this persecution, not prosecution." He saw this not just as a trial that might result in two years imprisonment and a $10,000 fine, but also as a case that could safeguard or endanger the rights of labor.

CLARENCE DARROW

Clarence Darrow. (Library of Congress)

Famed for his skills as an orator, Darrow is often best remembered for his stirring defense in what became known as the 1925 Scopes Monkey Trial, or, more properly, *Tennessee v. John Scopes,* in which John T. Scopes, a Tennessee high school teacher, was tried on charges that he violated state law by teaching evolution. Darrow met a prosecution headed by William Jennings Bryan in one of the most intently watched cases in American history. Though Scopes was eventually convicted, Darrow argued brilliantly for the defense, showcasing his rhetorical skills and sowing doubt in the public's mind about the wisdom of having a fundamentalist interpretation of the Bible guide school curriculum.

Darrow was born in Ohio in 1857 and was working as a lawyer for a railroad when he was offered the chance to defend Debs and other American Railway Union leaders in the Pullman trial. He quit his job to take the case and went on to become a nationally recognized defense attorney, tackling even the most hopeless of cases. Darrow was a staunch opponent of the death penalty and took great personal comfort in the fact that not a single client of his was ever sentenced to death. A lively and entertaining figure, especially in the courtroom, Darrow had a brilliant legal mind and a knack for theater. His courtroom summations were often poetic in nature, and he never lost sight of the larger philosophical issues behind his cases. A stalwart defender of the underdog, Darrow died in 1938, having left an indelible imprint on the law—and society—of his time.

Darrow argued that the general managers were the ones guilty of obstructing the United States mail. They wanted to use the public inconvenience of interrupted mail service as a club to beat back the workingmen and women fighting for better conditions. He produced the minutes of a General Managers' Association meeting as evidence of conspiracy to reduce wages.

Debs was the chief witness at his own trial. He presented the history and goals of the American Railway Union. He testified that he believed in strict obedience to the law and that he condemned all violence.

Then something strange happened. One of the jury members became ill and left. The judge ruled that adding a replacement at this time would probably not be legal. Darrow argued against this because he sensed that the jury was eleven to one to acquit Debs. He was probably right, for a year later the district attorney entered in the records "nolle prosequi," the legal term from Latin

George Pullman had great ambitions for the workers at his company, but his stubborn insistence on controlling their lives led to frustration and distrust. (Courtesy of the Newberry Library's Pullman Collection, Chicago.)

meaning "unwilling to prosecute." The judge refused to replace the juror, and the trial was never resumed. Still, this denied Debs his right to be found not guilty by jury, which would have greatly improved his reputation.

While Debs served the rest of his jail term for the earlier contempt conviction, he read and thought about economic systems. During this period, he committed himself to socialism and to the betterment of life for workers in a democracy.

Upon his release from Woodstock, American workers greeted Debs as a hero. In the following years, he ran for the United States presidency four times as a nominee of the Socialist Party of America.

When George Pullman died suddenly of a heart attack in 1897, Eugene Debs commented only, "Peace be to his ashes. Mr. Pullman would not arbitrate when he had 'nothing to arbitrate.' He is on an equality with toilers now."

7.
The Commission's Report

In 1888, six years before the Pullman Strike, Congress passed the Arbitration Act. This legislation guaranteed that Congress would provide mediators to arbitrate conflicts between groups that asked for such help. It also agreed to set up fact-finding commissions for labor-management disputes if a governor or the U.S. president requested such a commission.

On July 26, 1894, President Cleveland took advantage of this act to appoint three chairmen to inquire into the recent controversies between the Illinois Central and Rock Island railroads and their employees. He instructed the commission to take testimonies from all those who wished to give them. Carroll D. Wright, United States commissioner of labor, was assigned to the commission. Wright was a distinguished statistician from New Jersey

Carroll D. Wright, chairman of the commission that investigated the Pullman Strike. (Library of Congress)

and had organized the Bureau of Labor Statistics to provide objective research on labor problems. Nicholas E. Worthington, a lawyer and former congressman from Illinois, and John D. Kernan, from New York, were chosen as the other chairmen.

The Pullman Strike hearings began on August 15, 1894, in the Chicago post office, and lasted for two weeks. The commission spent another day in Washington, DC, on September 26. Any citizen or organization who wished to testify could do so. If they could not be present, they could send in their testimony in writing. One hundred and nine witnesses were heard by the three commissioners, who followed up the testimonies with questions.

PULLMAN COMPANY STATEMENT

In addition to hearing testimony from workers, the Strike Commission invited George Pullman and his company to give a statement. What follows is an excerpt.

In view of the proposed attempt of the American Railway Union to interfere with public travel on railway lines using Pullman cars, in consequence of a controversy as to the wages of employees of the manufacturing department of the company, the Pullman company requests the publication of the following statement of the facts, in face of which the attempt is to be made. . . .

[George Pullman, speaking to the union, said:] I can only assure you that if this company now restores the wages of the first half of 1893, as you have asked, it would be a most unfortunate thing for the men, because there is less than sixty days of contract work in sight in the shops under all orders and there is absolutely no possibility, in the present condition of affairs throughout the country, of getting any more orders for work at prices measured by the wages of May, 1893. Under such a scale the works would necessarily close down and the great majority of the employees be put in idleness, a contingency I am using my best efforts to avoid.

To further benefit the people of Pullman and vicinity we concentrated all the work that we could command at that point, by closing our Detroit shops entirely and laying off a large number of men at our other repair shops, and gave to Pullman the repair of all cars that could be taken care of there.

Also, for the further benefit of our people at Pullman we have carried on a large system of internal improvements, having expended nearly $160,000 since August last in work which, under normal conditions, would have been spread over one or two years. The policy would be to continue this class of work to as great an extent as possible, provided, of course, the Pullman men show a proper appreciation of the situation by doing whatever they can to help themselves to tide over the hard times which are so seriously felt in every part of the country.

There has been some complaint made about rents. As to this I would say that the return to this company on the capital invested in the Pullman tenements for the last year and the year before was 3.82 per cent. There are hundreds of tenements in Pullman renting for from $6 to $9 per month, and the tenants are relieved from the usual expenses of exterior cleaning and the removal of garbage, which is done by the company. The average amount collected from employees for gas consumed is about $2 a month. To ascertain the exact amount of water used by tenants, separate from the amount consumed by the works, we have recently put in meters, by which we find that the water consumed by the tenants, if paid for at the rate of 4 cents per 1,000 gallons, in accordance with our original contract with the village of Hyde Park, would amount to about $1,000 a month, almost exactly the rate which we have charged the tenants, this company assuming the expense of pumping. At the increased rate the city is now charging us for water we are paying about $500 a month in excess of the amount charged to the tenants. The present pay rolls at Pullman amount to about $7,000 a day.

On the question of rents, while, as stated above, they make a manifestly inadequate return upon the investment, so that it is clear they are not, in fact, at an arbitrarily high figure, it may be added that it would not be possible in a business sense so to deal with them.

The renting of the dwellings and the employment of workmen at Pullman are in no way tied together. The dwellings and apartments are offered for rent in competition with those of the immediately adjacent towns of Kensington, Roseland, and Gano. They are let alike to Pullman employees and to very many others in no way connected with the company, and, on the other hand, many Pullman employees rent or own their homes in those adjacent towns. The average rental at Pullman is at the rate of $3 per room per month. There are 1,200 tenements, of varying numbers of rooms, the average monthly rental of which is $10; of these there are 600 the average monthly rental of which is $8. In very many cases men with families pay a rent seemingly large for a workman, but which is in fact reduced in part, and often wholly repaid, by the subrents paid by single men as lodgers. . . .

The payrolls at the time [of the strike] amounted to about $7,000 a day, and were reduced $5,500 by the strike, so that during the period of a little more than six weeks which has elapsed the employees who quit their work have deprived themselves and their comrades of earnings of more than $200,000.

It is an element of the whole situation worthy of note that at the beginning of the strike the Pullman Savings Bank had on deposit in its savings department $488,000, of which about nine-tenths belonged to employees at Pullman, and that this amount has since been reduced by the sum of $32,000.

While deploring the possibility of annoyance to the public by the threats of irresponsible organizations to interrupt the orderly ministration to the comfort of travelers on railway lines, aggregating 125,000 miles in length, the Pullman company can do no more than explain its situation to the public. It has two separate branches of business, essentially distinct from each other. One is to provide sleeping cars, which are delivered by it under contract to the various railway companies, to be run by them on their lines as a part of their trains for the carriage of their passengers, over the movements of which this company has no control. Contract arrangements provide for the making of all repairs to such cars by the railway companies using them—as to certain repairs absolutely, and as to all others upon the request of the Pullman company, which ordinarily finds it most convenient to use its own manufacturing facilities to make such repairs. The other, and a distinct branch of the business of the Pullman company, is the manufacture of sleeping cars for the above-mentioned use of railway companies and the manufacture for sale to railway companies of freight cars and ordinary passenger cars, and of street cars, and this business is almost at a standstill throughout the United States. . . .

It is now threatened by American Railway Union officials that railway companies using Pullman sleeping cars shall be compelled to deprive their passengers of sleeping-car accommodations, unless the Pullman company will agree to submit to arbitration the question as to whether or not it shall open its manufacturing shops at Pullman and operate them under a scale of wages which would cause a daily loss to it of one-fourth the wages paid. . . .

After hearing all the witnesses, the three men carefully prepared their report. It was fifty-four pages full of information, titled "Report on the Chicago Strike of June-July, 1894." The recorded testimony of witnesses was included in an additional 681-page appendix.

According to the recorded testimony, the railroads lost $685,308 in destroyed property during the strike. They lost about $4 million in business. Pullman strikers lost $350,000 in wages, and striking railroad workers lost about $1.4 million, with many employees "still adrift and losing wages." The money lost from the paralysis of the Chicago distribution center was, the report said, "very great" and "widely distributed."

Twelve people had been fatally shot during the course of the strike, 515 arrested by police for murder, arson, burglary, assault, and rioting. Seventy-one were arrested for obstruction of U.S. mail or conspiracy to restrain interstate trade. The commissioners went on to discuss other aspects of the strike that could not be so easily quantified. These elements that needed to be "thoroughly understood by the people and to be wisely and prudently treated by the government" were: 1) the eagerness of laborers to strike; 2) the determination by railroad management to crush the strike rather than look for a peaceful solution; 3) the occasion to burn, loot, and murder which a strike provides for disreputable persons not connected with the strike; 4) the changing of hardworking, law-abiding people into idlers and lawbreakers; 5) the suffering brought to many innocent families;

and 6) the changing of railroad yards, stations, and markets into dangerous, armed camps.

The commission's report also presented a section of facts about the Pullman Palace Car Company, the American Railway Union, and the General Managers' Association. Here the commissioners stated that they did not favor an industrial union like the American Railway Union because the complexity of its members' different training, skills, conditions, and pride tended to defeat rather than assist their common goals. They disliked the way people who built railway cars were united with those who operated the trains: "This mistake led the union into a strike purely sympathetic and aided to bring upon it a crushing and demoralizing defeat."

The commissioners condemned the General Managers' Association as illegal. They called it "an illustration of the persistent and shrewdly devised plans of corporations to overreach . . . and usurp powers and rights." By pooling and charting their wage scales they were fixing wages. The commissioners also stated that it was "arrogant and absurd" for the managers to refuse to negotiate with the union, and "that a different policy would have prevented the loss of life and great loss of property and wages occasioned by the strike."

The loss of business to the Pullman Company following the depression of 1893 was acknowledged as a cause for the layoffs and cuts in pay that Pullman had forced upon his workers. But the commissioners said the employees were unfairly made to bear the brunt of the loss.

While workers' wages fell an average of 25 percent, no salaries of officers, managers, or superintendents were lowered. Though the Pullman Company showed evidence that it sustained losses in order to keep workers employed, the commissioners thought otherwise:

> The evidence shows that it sought to keep running mainly for its own benefit as a manufacturer, that its plant might not rust, that its competitors might not invade its territory, that it might keep its cars in repair, that it might be ready for resumption when business revived with a live plant and competent help, and that its revenue from its tenements might continue.

The commission's report summarized the events leading to the Pullman workers' strike and the American Railway Union boycott. The subsequent strike by railroad employees was defined as a sympathetic one, with no grievances presented against railroads: "Throughout the strike, the strife was simply over handling Pullman cars, the men being ready to do their duty otherwise." This sympathy was promoted by the fear felt by many because of previous wage reductions, blacklisting, and the growing power of the General Managers' Association.

It was found that in some cases the strikers had broken their contracts with the railroads, most notably the Illinois Central, and had justified their actions as

STUPIDITY and GREED

AN IMPENDING DOWNFALL

—*Ram's Horn.*

This contemporary cartoon captures many people's attitude toward the Pullman Strike. To most Americans, both sides behaved foolishly. (Library of Congress)

"balancing wrongs." When union agents urged them on, disorders had flamed out of control.

The commissioners found that both the Pullman Company and the General Managers' Association had repeatedly turned down proposals for arbitration or peaceful settlement. The General Managers' Association

had also set up headquarters to hire replacement workers, give information to the press, complain to the police,
and maintain communications with all railroads.

It was found that the association also armed and paid
3,600 guards, whom they had asked the U.S. marshal to
deputize. These men were thus taking orders from the
railroads but exercising the power of the United States.

The report confirmed that some of the problems arose
because the city of Chicago had a large population of
out-of-work people, many of whom had been stranded
there after the depression of 1893. According to the
commission,

[the] mobs that took possession of railroad yards,
tracks, and crossings . . . that stoned, tipped over,
burned, and destroyed cars and stole their contents,
were, by general concurrence in the testimony,
composed generally of hoodlums, women, a low
class of foreigners, and recruits from the criminal
classes. Few strikers were recognized or arrested in
these mobs, which were without leadership, and
seemed simply bent upon plunder and destruction.

Railroad strikers were mainly responsible for "the
spiking and misplacing of switches, removing rails,
crippling of interlocking systems, the detaching, side
tracking, and derailing of cars and engines, placing of
coupling pins in engine machinery, blockading tracks
with cars, and attempts to detach and run in mail cars."

In the conclusion, the commissioners wrote, "Many impartial observers are reaching the view that much of the real responsibility for these disorders rests with the people themselves and with the Government for not adequately controlling monopolies and corporations, and for failing to reasonably protect the rights of labor and redress its wrongs."

However, the commission was also critical of the union resorting to a strike, saying strikes

> are war . . . and call for progress to a higher plane of education and intelligence in adjusting the relations of capital and labor. These barbarisms waste the products of both capital and labor, defy law and order, disturb society, intimidate capital, convert industrial paths where there ought to be plenty into highways of poverty and crime, bear as their fruit the arrogant flush of victory and the humiliating sting of defeat, and lead to preparations for greater and more destructive conflicts.

Finally, the commissioners made three major recommendations to be presented to President Cleveland and Congress in November 1894:

> 1. A permanent U.S. Strike Commission should be created to investigate disputes between railroads and their employees and to make recommendations that the railroads must obey. Both railroads and incorporated national trade unions involved shall

THE NATIONAL LABOR RELATIONS BOARD

The Strike Commission's recommendations showed the importance of arbitration. It wanted to establish a permanent strike commission to compel industries to obey its decisions until the time these could be ruled on by arbitration or legal appeals. The National Labor Relations Board (NLRB) set up by the Wagner Act of 1935 seeks to fulfill what the commissioners had in mind.

In some countries like New Zealand, Canada, Australia, and England, arbitration can be ordered by the government. In the United States, the government must persuade the parties to accept arbitration. The American Arbitration Association, formed in 1926, now has 7,000 members who can be called to help settle labor disputes.

send elected representatives to be temporary members during their controversy.

2. The individual states should provide: a) a system of arbitration like the one already in Massachusetts and b) legal standing to labor organizations. Contracts requiring workers not to join a labor organization or to leave them as a condition of employment should be illegal.

3. Employers should recognize labor organizations. Wages should be raised when economic conditions allow, and when they are reduced, the reasons should be given. Employers should consider employees as essential as money to business success, and should consult with them when appropriate.

The 681 pages of printed testimony provide fascinating reading. The format is like a play script, which gives the reader a feeling of being present at the hearing. Commissioners Wright, Kernan, and Worthington asked questions like good lawyers or police officers, careful to distinguish between fact and hearsay, addressing all witnesses with respect and dignity.

The reader feels the desperation of Pullman employees like Thomas Heathcoate (car builder), Jennie Curtis (seamstress), Theodore Rhodie (painter), and Mary Alice Wood (electrical department worker) as they describe the details of their humiliating poverty. At other times the reader feels the frightening presence of the mobs along the tracks in south Chicago.

The appendix includes passages from one reporter for the *Chicago Record* who had ridden as far as Hammond, Indiana, on Sunday, July 8. There he encountered a mob that had turned back several passenger trains. He recounted how one man directed others to throw ropes over the top of a Pullman car standing isolated on the track. Pulling in unison, the men rocked to overturn the car, while women and children gathered to watch. Just as the car was about to go over, a caboose and locomotive arrived with U.S. troops aboard. The troops fired without warning into the crowd. Everyone scattered and hid behind boxcars, but one man was killed. The reporter did not know this was the innocent carpenter looking for his son.

There was also testimony about the town of Pullman

Illinois National Guardsmen fire on Pullman Company strikers in this Harper's Weekly *illustration from 1894.* (Courtesy of the Granger Collection.)

and the extent to which it was indeed a "model." Jane Addams, superintendent of Hull House in Chicago, was devoted to making life better for the poor and had visited Pullman. Her impression was that room rentals were about 25 percent higher in Pullman than for comparable places in Chicago, as she told the commissioners:

> I know very well . . . the neighborhood of Polk and Halsted streets in the locality of the Hull House, and it seems to me the rents at Pullman are higher

In 1889, Illinois native Jane Addams, known as the "mother of social work," co-founded Hull House in Chicago, a settlement house that provided shelter for the neighborhood poor and functioned as a center of social reform. Addams received the Nobel Peace Prize in 1931. (Library of Congress)

Hull House was located at the corner of Polk and Halsted Streets on Chicago's west side. The immigrant-heavy Halsted Street neighborhood was, at that time, a slum, complete with overcrowded tenements, crime, disease, inadequate schools, inferior hospitals, and poor sanitation. (Library of Congress)

than the rents in that vicinity, which is a mile west. You can get two rooms [near Hull House] for $6, while the cheapest two rooms I saw at Pullman were $7.50, and most of them $8.50. They were cleaner there because the surroundings were cleaner, but other facilities were no better.

Addams had spent years living and working with poverty-stricken residents of Chicago, and she knew firsthand the horrible working conditions the poor were subject to. She was disappointed that Pullman would not negotiate with the union, but not surprised. Addams was also personally affected by the strike—trains from Chicago were delayed, and she had trouble getting to visit her dying sister. Later she said of the Pullman Strike: "A quick series of events had dispelled the good nature which in happier times envelops the ugliness of the industrial situation."

8.

Legacy

The Pullman Strike sparked a number of controversies. Mayors, governors, the attorney general, and the president of the United States not only participated in the action but also represented very different positions on how the strike should be handled. Newspaper reporting at the time was usually strongly on one side or the other, as was public opinion. Some of the issues raised by the strike are still debated today.

George Pullman had refused to accept arbitration with the elected representatives of his employees about their conditions and wages. He and Pullman vice president Thomas Wickes argued that union representation deprived the worker of his individual liberty, even when the individual worker had voted for fellow workers to speak for him. Pullman and Wickes claimed they were always willing to listen to any worker who made an appointment with them. Obviously the workers did not agree that this was always possible—or effective.

One of the main issues in American labor was establishing the place unions would occupy. Even as owners fought to keep unions out of their shops and to remove unions from the negotiating table, workers were becoming convinced that only unionization could help them achieve the reforms they demanded. In the years to come, unions would continue to become more powerful and effective tools.

In the official strike report, the commissioners said the Pullman Company was "behind the age" in denying labor organizations a "place or necessity in Pullman." Forty years after the Pullman Strike, the National Labor Relations Act of 1935 (also called the Wagner Act) established the right of workers to collectively bargain. Today, the National Labor Relations Board exists to oversee interactions between workers and management and to ensure the rights of both sides are protected.

The Pullman Strike eventually destroyed the American Railway Union, in part because its attempt at being a vertical union made it cumbersome. New unions continued to develop, and many of them joined large, protective, umbrella organizations like the American Federation of Labor (established 1886) or the Congress of Industrial Organizations (1935). In Chicago in 1905, Eugene Debs helped establish the Industrial Workers of the World (IWW), which accepted everyone regardless of skill, race, sex, or creed, ranging from migrant agricultural workers to coal miners. The IWW reflected the socialist philosophy Debs had come to embrace and set as its goal the overthrow of the capitalist system. IWW members, sometimes called Wobblies, refused collective bargaining, but instead relied on strikes, boycotts, and propaganda to spread their message. In his address to the founding convention, Debs made it clear that he believed the real fight was about economic class:

> I am much impressed by this proletarian gathering. I realize that I stand in the presence of those who in the past have fought, are fighting, and will continue to fight the battles of the working class economically and politically, until the capitalist system is overthrown and the working class are emancipated from all of the degrading thralldom of the ages. In this great struggle the working class are often defeated, but never vanquished. Even the defeats, if we are wise enough to profit by them, but hasten the day of the final victory.
>
> In taking a survey of the industrial field of today, we are at once impressed with the total inadequacy of working-class organization, with the lack of solidarity, with the widespread demoralization we see, and we are bound to conclude that the old form of pure and simple unionism has long since outgrown its usefulness; that it is now not only in

Debs, photographed here with railroad workers, stood in unity with America's working class throughout his life. (Eugene V. Debs Foundation, Terre Haute, Indiana)

the way of progress, but that it has become positively reactionary, a thing that is but an auxiliary of the capitalist class.

Industrial unions did not die out after the Pullman Strike. They continued to grow and reached peak power in the first half of the twentieth century. By 1960, 33 percent of all American workers belonged to unions. Union membership has been in steep decline since then. In 1990, only 16 percent of U.S. workers were unionized. The AFL and CIO merged in 1955, forming the AFL-CIO, an organization that is today about nine million members strong.

The Pullman Strike also raised questions about the necessity or appropriateness of the model town. Much of the suffering of the workers came about because they could not access their pay—rent and other costs were deducted directly from their paychecks. Pullman's refusal to lower rents or, as Governor Altgeld suggested, forgive them, in order to allow his workers to get back on their feet, turned public opinion strongly against Pullman and his company town.

Shortly after the strike ended, the attorney general of Illinois initiated court procedures to end the charter of the model town for violation of corporate rights. In other words, the Pullman Palace Car Company was authorized to build, lease, and sell railway cars, but not to acquire real estate holdings, or to establish and manage a town. Pullman officials argued that they had been counseled otherwise, and they had not been challenged for fifteen years. They believed that Governor Altgeld wanted to please labor organizations and was making the Pullman Company a victim to do so. They appealed the decision against Pullman to the Illinois Supreme Court in October 1898. The high court upheld the original decision and ordered Pullman to sell all property not necessary to manufacturing train cars within five years.

Since our country's earliest years, people have disagreed about the relationship between state and federal powers. Such disagreements were a major cause of the Civil War, which ended only twenty-nine years before the Pullman Strike.

Governor Altgeld of Illinois and the governors of Indiana, Colorado, Kansas, Missouri, Oregon, Idaho, and Texas felt the federal government had wrongly intervened in state matters. They protested to Cleveland and Olney. Altgeld later argued, "Local self-government is the very foundation of freedom and of republican institutions, and no people possess this who are subject to have the army patrol their streets, acting not under, but independently of the local authorities, and do this at the mere discretion of one man, or of a central power that is far away."

President Cleveland's use of the Army in Illinois without the governor's request surprised people. Cleveland was a Democrat, and at that time the Democratic Party publicly championed states' rights against the power of the federal government. It was the party most

President Grover Cleveland was an adamant opponent of labor union strikes, such as the Pullman Strike, that interfered with government activity or interstate commerce. This oil painting of Cleveland by Anders Zorn was made in 1899.

opposed to the growth of federal power. But Olney argued that "the soil of Illinois is the soil of the United States." Cleveland responded tersely to a lengthy telegram from Altgeld, writing:

> Sir: Federal Troops were sent to Chicago in strict accordance with the Constitution and laws of the United States, upon the demand of the post office department that obstruction of the mails should be removed, and upon the representations of the judicial officers of the United States that the process of the Federal courts could not be executed through the ordinary means, and upon competent proof that conspiracies existed against commerce between the States. To meet these conditions, which are clearly within the province of Federal authority, the presence of Federal troops in the city of Chicago was deemed not only proper, but necessary, and there has been no intention of thereby interfering with the plain duty of the local authorities to preserve the peace of the city.

Still, the use of federal force would be an issue in strikes to come, and the memory of Pullman would strongly impact those decisions.

One other source of controversy was the fact that President Grover Cleveland, Attorney General Richard Olney, and Judge Peter Grosscup had all been connected with railroads in their private law practices. Olney in particular was known as a railroad lawyer. But most lawyers of this era who had reached Olney's high position had represented railroads in the course of their careers, including Clarence Darrow, Debs's defense attorney. Though the law did tend to favor big business, it seems unlikely rank corruption was a factor in this case.

The Pullman Strike was a watershed moment in American labor history. When the Pullman workers went on strike, it set off a ripple effect that traveled through

Despite the disruption of the strike, the revocation of the town of Pullman's charter, and the eventual strengthening of the labor movement, the Pullman Palace Car Company continued to produce train cars far into the twentieth century. After George Pullman's death in 1897, Abraham Lincoln's son, Robert Todd Lincoln, took over as president of the company. (Library of Congress)

the railroads to other manufacturing and distribution businesses, and even to the federal government. Because it involved the huge American Railway Union, thousands of workers unrelated to the Pullman Company also went on strike.

The dispute also had national significance because railway owners succeeded in bringing in the power of the federal government on their side. The strategy of bringing in state and federal troops to break up strikes had long been the preferred tactic of industrialists. It had been used at McCormick Harvester in 1886, when the events at Haymarket caused such a stir, and at the Homestead Steel Works in 1892. But this time the tactic had ramifications beyond the immediate strike. Eventually, it would create a backlash against using militia paid for by taxpayers to take management's side during a strike.

The Pullman Strike occurred in the early years of what came to be called the Progressive Movement. Progressives advocated a more level playing field between labor and owners, as well as a number of social and political changes including electoral reform, women's suffrage, bank regulations, and an income tax. One of the Progressives' continued demands was for laws to be passed that limited the methods management could use to crush a strike, including a limit on injunctions. These laws would be a long time coming, but change was inevitable. By 1914, when President Woodrow Wilson sent federal troops in to a coal-mining strike near Ludlow, in southeastern Colorado, they were under strict orders not to take sides or to participate in any strikebreaking activities. Recognizing the potential for yet another labor-related uprising, Wilson aimed to keep the commotion in Ludlow to a peaceful minimum. Little did he know that he had stepped into what would become an intensely heated and violent situation, even as the U.S. was still feeling the repercussions of the Pullman Strike.

TIMELINE

1864-65	George Pullman patents and builds the Pioneer, the modern railroad sleeping car.
1867	Pullman founds the Pullman Palace Car Company.
1869	Knights of Labor is founded to represent all kinds of laborers.
1877	First major railroad strike is started by Baltimore & Ohio firemen after a 10 percent pay reduction; the strike spreads to other eastern railroads, collapsing when state and federal troops are called in.
1880-81	Pullman founds the town of Pullman south of Chicago on Lake Calumet as a model community for workers of his company.
1886	Knights of Labor is reorganized into the American Federation of Labor by Samuel Gompers; General Managers' Association is formed in Chicago by managers from twenty-four railroads to establish pay scales for railroad workers.
1893 May-Nov.	World's Columbian Exposition (also called the Chicago Fair) held in honor of four hundredth anniversary of Columbus's voyage; financial panic sweeps the country, paralyzing industry and causing three million workers to lose jobs while millions more see their wages cut.
June 20	American Railway Union is founded to unite rail

way workers in a single organization; Eugene Debs is elected its president; wages in Pullman Works are greatly reduced by 25 percent average from September 1893 to May 1894.

1894

March-May	Some Pullman workers join the American Railway Union.
April	Debs leads successful American Railway Union strike against the Great Northern; a committee of Minneapolis-St. Paul businessmen arbitrates in favor of the workers.
May 7-9	A committee of Pullman workers asks for increased wages and lower rents in Pullman housing.
May 10	Three members of the committee are laid off; forty-six representatives of the local union for Pullman workers call for a strike vote.
May 11	4,000 workers of the Pullman Palace Car Company strike to protest wage cuts and the perceived firing of union representatives.
June 12-23	The American Railway Union holds a convention in Chicago, representing 150,000 members.
June 15-22	Pullman Company refuses communication with the ARU and consideration of any arbitration.
June 21	Delegates of the ARU vote to stop handling Pullman cars on June 26 if Pullman Company refuses arbitration.
June 22	Pullman Company meets with General Managers' Association and decides to resist the boycott on handling Pullman cars.
June 26	A boycott and accompanying strikes begin and spread as General Managers' Association members discharge men who refuse to handle passenger

	trains with Pullman cars.
June 28	Complaints of forcible seizures of trains and other violence cause U.S. attorney general Richard Olney to order U.S. district attorneys to arrest any people engaged in obstruction of trains.
June 30	Chicago district attorney reports disabled mail trains and recommends deputizing of guards to ride the mail trains; Olney suggests application of Sherman Antitrust Act of 1890 to break the strike in Chicago as a conspiracy.
July 2	Olney has the Chicago district attorney issue an injunction to Eugene Debs and the American Railway Union, forbidding the restraint of interstate commerce, the obstruction of the U.S. mail, and the coercion of nonstriking railway workers; U.S. Army troops at Fort Sheridan prepare to move to Chicago.
July 3	In Chicago, U.S. marshal J. W. Arnold reports mobs detaching mail cars, overturning freight cars, controlling railway junctions, etc., and asks for the troops.
July 4	Federal troops arrive in Chicago.
July 5	A mob of 2,000 is reported at the Chicago Stock Yards, milling among the troops, obstructing traffic, and derailing a train; Governor Altgeld requests removal of federal troops in a telegram to President Cleveland, declaring state troops are in adequate control; Altgeld protests federal supremacy over states' rights; buildings in Jackson Park left from the Chicago Fair are set afire.
July 6	Over 700 box cars are burned in the rail yards at Fiftieth Street; a mob stones and shoots at soldiers and crew on a train clearing an obstruction; Illinois militia use bayonets and bullets to break up the

mob; four are killed, twenty wounded.

July 8	President Cleveland issues an executive proclamation to Chicago for people to cease troublemaking.
July 10	A federal grand jury finds "conspiracy to obstruct the US mails;" Debs and three others are arrested; militia opens up blockade to the Chicago Stock Yards.
July 12	American Railway Union offers to abandon the strike and boycott if workers are rehired.
July 13	Chicago rail yards are all open and train schedules back to normal; American Railway Union representatives meet with American Federation of Labor officials and conclude the strike is lost; they advise workers to return to work and seek remedy by voting for political candidates sympathetic to labor.
July 17	Debs is arrested a second time for contempt of court in violating the July 2 injunction.
July 18	Strikers allowed to return to work at Pullman if they agree not to belong to a union.
July 26	President Cleveland appoints a committee to collect and report the facts about the strike.
August 15	Hearings of the U.S. Strike Commission begin in Chicago.
November 14	"Report on the Chicago Strike of June-July, 1894" by the United States Strike Commission presented to President Cleveland; it condemns boycotts, lockouts, and strikes, and says that the "real responsibility for these disorders rests with the people themselves and with the Government for not adequately controlling monopolies and corporations, and for failing to reasonably protect the rights of labor and redress its wrongs."
December 14	Debs and associates are found guilty of contempt of court.

1895

January 8	Debs begins six-month jail sentence for contempt.
January 14	Debs appeals to the Supreme Court.
January 24	Debs's conspiracy trial begins in Chicago.
February 12	A juror gets sick, and the judge rules he cannot be replaced; the conspiracy trial is never resumed by the prosecution.
May 27	*In re Debs* decision: Supreme Court upholds the right of the U.S. Government to use injunctions and physical force in preventing obstruction of U.S. mail and interstate commerce.
1898	Illinois Supreme Court says that the town of Pullman, where all property belongs to a single company, is a problem and orders Pullman Company to sell within five years all property not a part of their factory.
1901	Various socialist wings are united in the Socialist Party of America (with Debs as presidential candidate in 1904, 1908, 1912, and 1920).

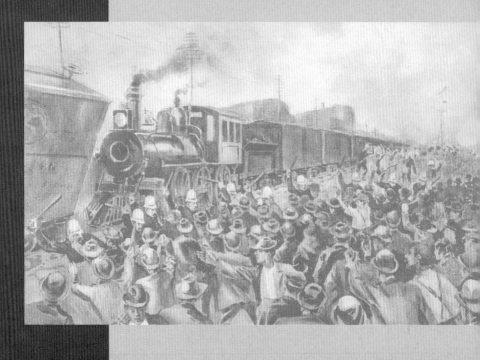

GLOSSARY

anarchy: from Greek meaning "without a ruler," this word refers to a society in which no one rules, and all do as they think best. Anarchists are people who strongly reject any established government and often work to overthrow it by violent means.

arbitration: the settlement of a dispute by a person chosen to hear both sides and come to a judgment the disputants agree in advance to follow.

bail: money deposited in a court of law to guarantee that an arrested person will show up for trial. The larger the alleged crime, the greater the bail will be. The money is returned after the trial.

blacklist: a list of persons considered troublemakers; an employer who values the list will refuse to hire anyone on it. For example, workers dismissed by their railroad for being involved in a strike were not hired by another railroad.

boycott: a large organized refusal to support a person, place, or thing. The word comes from the name of a cruel landlord's agent in nineteenth-century Ireland, Charles Boycott; the people would not look at him or talk to him, making him ineffective and causing him to lose his job.

civil court: trial procedure for the resolution of private disputes, such as family problems and contract violations.

criminal court: trial procedure for one accused of violating specific laws that harm others or threaten public safety. The Sixth Amendment of the U.S. Constitution guarantees an impartial jury trial for one brought to trial for a criminal offense.

contempt of court: an act judged to show disrespect for the authority or dignity of a court of law. This includes disobedience of a court order outside of the courtroom and unruly behavior or dress within the court room.

equity court: trial procedure by lawyers and judges for interpreting and applying law in civil cases upon principles of fairness and according to previous applications called precedents. Equity cases differ from civil cases because relief (the starting or stopping of an action) is sought rather than a payment of money.

grand jury: a jury, usually more than twelve, that investigates accusations and evidence to determine if the accused should be brought to trial before a petit jury of twelve citizens. *Grand* and *petit* are French words that mean large and small.

indict: to make a legal accusation, bringing a person to trial, usually said of a grand jury. An indictment refers to the accusation itself. The pronunciation is not phonetic; it is pronounced *in-dight,* to rhyme with "in light."

injunction: an order from a court of law forbidding or ordering an action. Disobedience of an injunction is considered contempt of court.

layoff: temporary unemployment. A worker expects rehiring when the company can resume full production.

lockout: a refusal by an employer to let workers into the workplace until problems are resolved.

militia: citizens and former soldiers trained for emergency service in their states. The militia can be ordered by the governor to keep order in the state, or by the president to help in a national emergency. The combined state militias are called the National Guard.

monopoly: complete control of a certain kind of goods or service. The word comes from the Greek, meaning "one place only" (to buy things or get a service.) Historically, when large railroads bought up smaller ones, people had no competing railroad from whom they could get cheaper rates.

strike: an organized refusal by employees to work unless certain demands are met, usually having to do with wages, hours, or working conditions.

subpoena: an order from a court of law to a person to appear in the court to give testimony. A subpoena is always written and delivered in person. It comes from the Latin phrase "with punishment," and indicates that if a person does not come, he or she may be charged with contempt of court. Pronounced *suh-'pee-nah.*

SOURCES

CHAPTER ONE: The Chicago Strike

p. 15, "unusual and especially perplexing," Grover Cleveland. *The Government in the Chicago Strike of 1894: The Problem of Federal Intervention* (Princeton: Princeton University Press, 1913), 1.

CHAPTER THREE: A Company Town

p. 35, "[The workers] want . . ." Almont Lindsey, *The Pullman Strike: The Story of a Unique Experiment and of a Great Labor Upheaval* (Chicago: The University of Chicago Press, 1942), 65.

p. 35-36, "Here is a population . . ." David Papke, *The Pullman Case: The Clash of Labor and Capital in Industrial America* (Lawrence: The University Press of Kansas, 1999), 14.

p. 36, "un-American . . . the repression of all freedom," Ibid.

p. 36, "the consideration of problems . . ." Lindsey, *The Pullman Strike,* 115.

CHAPTER FOUR: The Strike Spreads

p. 42-43, "My family consists . . ." Leon Stein, ed. *The Pullman Strike* (New York: Arno & The New York Times, 1969), 104-105.

p. 43, "I believe a rich . . ." Lindsey, *The Pullman Strike,* 124.

p. 44, "from a bottle . . ." William Carwardine, *The Pullman Strike* (Chicago, Kerr, 1894), 43.

p. 44, "The American flag . . ." Ibid., 46.

p. 45, "Mr. President and Brothers . . ." Jennie Curtis, "Address to 1894 Convention of American Railway Union," Illinois Labor History Society, http://www.kentlaw.edu/ilhs/ jennie.htm (September 21, 2005).

p. 47, "nothing to arbitrate," Lindsey, *The Pullman Strike,* 129.

p. 51, "mail trains . . ." Ibid., 161-162.

p. 52-54, "and all persons combining . . ." Colston E. Warne, ed., *The Pullman Boycott of 1894* (Boston: D. C. Heath and Company, 1955) 31-32.

p. 54-55, "Gatling gun on paper . . ." Lindsey, *The Pullman Strike,* 162.

p. 55, "a desperate time . . . inadequate force," Ibid., 164.

p. 55, "impossible to move . . ." Ibid.

p. 57, "have in some . . ." Ibid., 186.

p. 57-58, "To absolutely ignore . . ." Ibid., 187.

CHAPTER FIVE: A Chain Reaction

p. 65-71, "August 16, 1894 . . ." "Testimony on the Part of Striking Employees: Testimony by Theodore Rhodie," Chicago Public Library, http://www.chipublib.org/003cpl/hf/ pullman_strike5.html (September 28, 2005).

CHAPTER SIX: Debs Goes to Jail

p. 81, "We have assurance . . ." Lindsey, *The Pullman Strike,* 268.

p. 81-85, "Kensington, Ill., August 17, 1894. . . ." American Social History Project, "Broken Spirits: Letters on the Pull man Strike," George Mason University, http:// historymatters.gmu.edu/d/5363/ (September 28, 2005).

p. 86, "an agreement . . ." Lindsey, *The Pullman Strike,* 278.

p. 87, "The poor striker . . ." Papke, *The Pullman Case,* 44.

p. 88, "public nuisance," Lindsey, *The Pullman Strike,* 297.

p. 89, "If emergency arises . . ." Ibid.
p. 90, "The entire strength . . ." Papke, *The Pullman Case,* 75.
p. 91, "puppet in the . . ." Lindsey, *The Pullman Strike,* 301.
p. 94, "Peace be to . . ." Ibid., 342.

CHAPTER SEVEN: The Commission's Report
p. 97-100, "In view of the . . ." Warne, *The Pullman Boycott of 1894,* 14-17.
p. 101, "still adrift and losing wages," Ibid., 7.
p. 101, "very great . . . widely distributed," Ibid.
p. 101, "thoroughly understood by . . ." Ibid., 8.
p. 102, "This mistake led . . ." Ibid., 11.
p. 102, "an illustration of . . ." Papke, *The Pullman Case,* 81.
p. 102, "arrogant and absurd," Ibid., 82.
p. 102, "that a different . . ." Ibid.
p. 103, "The evidence shows . . ." Warne, *The Pullman Boycott of 1894,* 20.
p. 103, "Throughout the strike . . ." Ibid., 23.
p. 104, "balancing wrongs," Ibid.
p. 105, "[the] mobs that took . . ." Ibid., 25.
p. 105, "the spiking and . . ." Ibid.
p. 106, "Many impartial observers . . ." Ibid., 26.
p. 106-107, "are war . . ." Lindsey, *The Pullman Strike,* 354.
p. 109, 111, "I know very well . . ." "Miscellaneous Testimony: Testimony of Jane Addams," Chicago Public Library, http://www.chipublib.org/003cpl/hf/pullman_strike8.html (September 28, 2005).
p. 112, "A quick series . . ." Papke, *The Pullman Case,* 37.

CHAPTER EIGHT: Legacy
p. 114, "behind the age . . . in Pullman," Warne, *The Pullman Boycott of 1894,* 11.
p. 115, 117, "I am much impressed . . ." Debs, Eugene V, *Eugene*

V. Debs Speaks ed Jean Y. Tussey (New York: Pathfinder Press, 1970), 112.

p. 118, "Local self-government . . ." Warne, *The Pullman Boycott of 1894,* 51.

p. 120, "the soil of Illinois . . ." Ibid., 80.

p. 120, "Sir: Federal Troops . . ." Ibid., 49.

BIBLIOGRAPHY

American Social History Project. "Broken Spirits: Letters on the Pullman Strike." George Mason University. http://historymatters.gmu.edu/d/5363/.

Biographical Directory of the U.S. Congress 1774-1971. Washington: U.S. Government Printing Office, 1971.

Carwardine, William H. *The Pullman Strike.* Chicago: Charles Kerr, 1894. Authorized facsimile. Ann Arbor, MI: University Microfilms, 1969.

Cleveland, Grover. *The Government in the Chicago Strike of 1894.* Princeton, NJ: Princeton University Press, 1913.

Curtis, Jennie. "Address to 1894 Convention of American Railway Union." Illinois Labor History Society. http://www.kentlaw.edu/ilhs/jennie.htm.

Debs, Eugene V. *Eugene V. Debs Speaks.* Edited by Jean Y. Tussey. New York: Pathfinder Press, 1970.

———. *Liberty: A Speech Delivered at Battery D Chicago, on Release from Woodstock Jail,* November 22, 1895. Terre Haute, IN: E. V. Debs & Co., 1895.

Edwards, Paul K. *Strikes in the U.S. 1881-1974.* Oxford, UK: Basil Blackwell, 1981.

Howard, Robert P. *Mostly Good and Competent Men: Illinois Governors 1818-1988.* Springfield, IL: Illinois State Historical Society, 1988.

Husband, Joseph. *The Story of the Pullman Car.* Chicago: A. C. McClurg, 1917.

King, Willard L. "The Debs Case." Lecture at Amherst College, November 19, 1952.

Lewis, Oscar. *The Big Four.* New York: Knopf, 1941.

Lindsey, Almont. *The Pullman Strike: The Story of a Unique Experiment and of a Great Labor Upheaval.* Chicago: University of Chicago Press, 1942.

Manning, Thomas G. *The Chicago Strike of 1894: Industrial Labor in the Late Nineteenth Century.* New York: Holt, Rinehart and Winston, 1965.

"Miscellaneous Testimony: Testimony of Jane Addams." Chicago Public Library. http://www.chipublib.org/003cpl/hf/pullman_strike8.html.

Myers, Gustavus. *History of the Supreme Court of the United States.* Chicago: Charles H. Kerr, 1912.

Paddock, Lisa. *Facts about the Supreme Court of the United States.* New York: H. H. Wilson, 1996.

Papke, David. *The Pullman Case: The Clash of Labor and Capital in Industrial America.* Lawrence, KS: The University Press of Kansas, 1999.

Renstrom, Peter G. *The American Law Dictionary.* Santa Barbara, CA: ABC-CLIO, 1991.

Stein, Leon, ed. *The Pullman Strike.* New York: Arno & The New York Times, 1969.

"Testimony on the Part of Striking Employees: Testimony by Theodore Rhodie." Chicago Public Library. http://www.chipublib.org/003cpl/hf/pullman_strike5.html.

United States Strike Commission. "Report on the Chicago Strike of June-July, 1894." Washington: Government

Printing Office, 1895. Facsimile Reprint. Clifton, NJ:
Augustus M. Kelley Publishers, 1972.
Warne, Colston E., ed. *The Pullman Boycott of 1894: The
Problem of Federal Intervention.* Boston: D. C. Heath and
Company, 1955.

WEB SITES

**http://www.pbs.org/newshour/bb/business/september96/
labor_day_9-2.html**
This PBS site explains the relationship between the Pullman
Strike and the creation of Labor Day.

http://www.eugenevdebs.com/
Though he died in 1926, Eugene Debs lives on via this
informative and picture-laden Web site.

http://www.aflcio.org/
Labor unions continue to be an important part of the American
economy. In 1955, the AFL merged with another union, the
Congress of Industrial Organizations, to form the AFL-CIO,
which is today nine million members strong.

http://www.iww.org/en/node
The Industrial Workers of the World, a radical union, continues
to advocate for the abolition of the wage system.

http://www.nlrb.gov/nlrb/home/default.asp
The National Labor Relations Board was created in 1935 to oversee the interaction between private corporations and their employees and/or unions.

http://www.scsra.org/library/porter.html
The Southern California Scenic Railway Association has re-printed an interesting history of the Pullman porter.

INDEX

Addams, Jane, 40, 109-112, *110*

Altgeld, John P., 22-25, *23, 24,* 56-58, 81-85, 117-118, 120

American Federation of Labor (AFL), 19-20, 114, 117

American Railway Union (ARU), 21, 44-49, 52, 61, 64, 72-73, 76, 79, 81, 86, 88, 90-92, 100, 102-103, 114, 122

Arbitration Act, 95

Arnold, J. W., 51, 55-56

Atchison, F., 44

Atchison, Topeka & Santa Fe Railroad, 36, 47, 64

Baltimore & Ohio Railroad, 18, 36

Brennan, Michael, 56

Brotherhood of Sleeping Car Porters, 31

Bryan, William Jennings, 91

Carnegie, Andrew, 34

Carnegie Steel Corporation, 18-19

Carwardine, William, 44

Central Pacific Railroad, 74-75, *74*

Chicago & Alton Railroad, 29

Chicago, Burlington & Quincy Railroad, 36

Chicago & Northwestern Railroad, 36, 47

Chicago & Rock Island Railroad, 36, 95

Chicago's World Fair, 39-40, *40,* 58-59

Civil War, 15, 16-17, 22, 118

Cleveland, Grover, 15, 40, *40,* 49-50, 56-58, 61, 72-73, 75, 95, 106, 118-120, *119*

Commonwealth v. Hunt, 17

Congress of Industrial Organizations (CIO), 114, 117

Curtis, Jennie, 45, 108

Darrow, Clarence, 90-92, *91,* 121

Debs, Eugene V., 20-22, *20,* 26, 43-44, 46, *46,* 51, 52, 54, 80, 86-92, *87,* 94, 114-116, *116,* 121

Douglass, Frederick, 40

Egan, John, 48, 57

Ely, Richard, 35-36

Franklin, Benjamin, 77, *77*

General Managers' Association, 36-37, 92, 102-104

Gilbert, James, 56

Gompers, Samuel, 19

Great Northern Railroad, 21-22

Great Northern strike, 22

Gregory, Stephen Strong, 91

Grosscup, Peter, 86, 90, 120

Haymarket Square riots, 18, 24-25, 122

Heathcoate, Thomas, 108

Hill, James J., 21

Homestead riot, 19, *19,* 122

Hopkins, John, 56

Hull House, 109-111, *111*

Illinois Central Railroad, 36, 47, 58-59, *58,* 95, 103

Industrial Workers of the World (IWW), 114-115

In re Debs, 89

Interstate Commerce Act, 51

Kernan, John D., 67, 69, 97, 101, 108

Lamont, Daniel, 49

Lincoln, Abraham, 29, 121

Lincoln, Robert Todd, 121

Ludlow Coal strike, 122-123

Milchrist, Thomas, 51

Missouri Pacific Railroad, 64

National Labor Relations Board, 107, 114

Newell, L. J., 82

Northern Pacific Railroad, 76, *76*

Olney, Richard, 49-51, *50,* 55-57, 73, 75-76, 89, 118, 120-121

Pollans, F. E., 82

Pony Express, 77

Pullman, George M., 12, 26-29, *27,* 32, 34-36, 42, 47, 81-85, *93,* 94, 113, 121

Pullman Palace Car Company,

11, 14, *14,* 29, *32,* 33-34, 39, 44-45, 47-49, 60, 79, 80-85, 90, 100, 102-104, 117-118, 121
Pullman Strike, *10, 14, 55, 60, 62, 104, 109*

Randolph, A. Philip, 31, *31*
Rhodie, Theodore, 65-71, 82, 108

Schofield, John, 49, 56
Sherman Antitrust Act of 1890, 51, 73
Southern Pacific Railroad, 73-74

Tennessee v. John Scopes (Scopes Monkey Trial), 91
Tesla, Nikola, 40

Union Pacific Railroad, 72
U.S. Strike Commision Report, 65-71, 97-108

Wagner Act of 1935, 107, 114
Wickes, Thomas, 45, 47, 113-114
Wilson, Woodrow, 122
Wood, Mary Alice, 108
Worthington, Nicholas, 69-71, 97, 101, 108

Wright, Caroll D., 65-66, 68-71, 95-97, *96,* 101, 108